REVISE PEARSON EDEXCE
GCSE (9–1)
Biology

GRADES 7–9
Revision & Practice

Series consultant: Harry Smith
Author: Sue Kearsey

Also available to support your revision:

Revise GCSE Study Skills Guide 9781292318875

The **Revise GCSE Study Skills Guide** is full of tried-and-trusted hints and tips for how to learn more effectively. It gives you techniques to help you achieve your best – throughout your GCSE studies and beyond.

Revise GCSE Revision Planner 9781292318868

The **Revise GCSE Revision Planner** helps you to plan and organise your time, step-by-step, throughout your GCSE revision. Use this book and wall chart to mastermind your revision.

For the full range of Pearson revision titles across KS2, KS3, GCSE, Functional Skills, AS/A Level and BTEC visit:
www.pearsonschools.co.uk/revise

Contents

Use this quick quiz to check that you are confident with the core skills and knowledge you need for the Pearson Edexcel GCSE (9-1) Biology Higher exam or Combined Science Higher exam.

Check your understanding with solutions to all the exam-style questions.

Welcome to Nail it!

This book provides revision and practice to help you nail down a top grade in your Pearson Edexcel GCSE (9–1) Biology Higher exam or Combined Science Higher exam. Designed for students aiming for a grade 7, 8 or 9, it is packed with exam tips, support for tricky topics, and exam-style practice questions to make sure you are ready to tackle the toughest questions and achieve top marks.

For more help with these topics, check out these pages in the Revise Pearson Edexcel GCSE (9–1) Biology Higher Revision Guide. To check out pages in the Revise Pearson Edexcel GCSE (9–1) Combined Science Higher Revision Guide, see the table on page 73.

Track your progress by ticking these boxes.

Worked example exam-style questions show you exactly how to tackle tricky questions and set out your working.

Knowledge check hints give you reminders of key information and core skills. You need to be confident with these to help you achieve that top grade.

Support in bringing in knowledge from other topics to enhance your answer is given in the synoptic links.

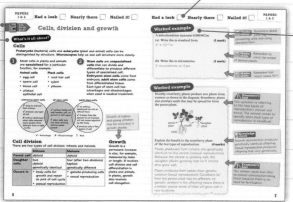

Revise the key facts for this topic.

Check that you are on track for a top grade with these exam-style questions. There are answers at the back of the book.

Reminders of any maths skills needed to answer a question.

Examiner's hints give top tips for exam success.

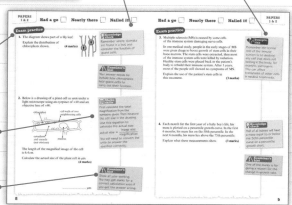

Knowledge check

If you are aiming for a top grade, you need to be confident with core skills and knowledge, such as knowing about cell structure, being able to name the parts of the eye and knowing how disease is spread. Take this quick quiz to find out which skills and knowledge you might need to brush up on before tackling the topics in this book. Answers are on page 66.

Revise core skills

Use the **Revise Pearson Edexcel GCSE (9–1) Biology Revision Guide** if you need to revise any of the core skills. The green arrows tell you which pages in the Guide to look at for more help with each of the topics covered in the quiz.

1. Which of these cells does not contain a nucleus?

   ☐ **A** plant cell

   ☐ **B** bacterial cell

   ☐ **C** animal cell

   ☐ **D** algal cell

2. Which cell structure carries out respiration?

   ....

3. Which cell structure is found in plant cells but not animal cells?

   ☐ **A** cell wall

   ☐ **B** cell membrane

   ☐ **C** mitochondrion

   ☐ **D** ribosome

4. What is the magnification of a microscope when using a ×5 eyepiece and a ×40 objective?

   ☐ **A** ×8   ☐ **B** ×20

   ☐ **C** ×100   ☐ **D** ×200

5. What is 1 micrometre written in standard form?

   ☐ **A** 1×10^{-2} m   ☐ **B** 1×10^{-3} m

   ☐ **C** 1×10^{-6} m   ☐ **D** 1×10^{-9} m

6. Why are enzymes called catalysts?

   ....

7. Which subunits are proteins synthesised from?

   ☐ **A** amino acids

   ☐ **B** sugars

   ☐ **C** carbohydrates

   ☐ **D** fatty acids and glycerol

8. Which reagent is used to test for the presence of protein in food?

   ☐ **A** iodine solution

   ☐ **B** Benedict's reagent

   ☐ **C** biuret reagent

   ☐ **D** ethanol

9. What does a calorimeter measure?

   ....

10. A cell is placed in a solution that has a lower solute concentration. In which direction will diffusion of solute molecules occur?

- ☐ **A** out of the cell into the solution
- ☐ **B** into the cell from the solution
- ☐ **C** in both directions at once
- ☐ **D** no diffusion will take place

11. How do water molecules enter a plant?

- ☐ **A** osmosis into root hair cells
- ☐ **B** active transport into root hair cells
- ☐ **C** diffusion into leaf cells
- ☐ **D** osmosis into leaf cells

12. Which part of the brain controls basic functions such as heart and breathing rate?

- ☐ **A** cerebral hemispheres
- ☐ **B** cerebellum
- ☐ **C** medulla oblongata
- ☐ **D** all of the above

13. Which type of neurone is only found in the brain and spinal cord (CNS)?

....

14. Which part of a neurone insulates it from other neurones?

....

15. Which part of the eye changes shape to focus a near object clearly?

- ☐ **A** the cornea
- ☐ **B** the iris
- ☐ **C** the lens
- ☐ **D** the retina

16. In which cells does meiosis take place? 27

- ☐ **A** all body cells
- ☐ **B** embryonic stem cells
- ☐ **C** gametes
- ☐ **D** gamete-producing cells

17. What links the two strands in a molecule of DNA? 28

- ☐ **A** bonds between sugars on each strand
- ☐ **B** bonds between phosphates on each strand
- ☐ **C** bonds between bases on each strand
- ☐ **D** no bonds, the strands just coil together

18. What is the definition of a genome? 28

....

19. Which cell structure is important in protein synthesis? 29

- ☐ **A** mitochondrion
- ☐ **B** cytoplasm
- ☐ **C** ribosome
- ☐ **D** chloroplast

20. What is an allele? 31

....

21. If R is the allele for red flowers and r is the allele for white flowers, what colour will the flowers be for a plant that is Rr (assuming no codominance)? 32

....

3

22. Which of these human characteristics is caused by genetic variation?

- [ ] **A** length of trimmed fingernails
- [ ] **B** dyed hair colour
- [ ] **C** shape of face
- [ ] **D** none of the above

23. What causes natural selection?

- [ ] **A** humans choosing which organisms to breed
- [ ] **B** evolution
- [ ] **C** variation in survival due to the environment
- [ ] **D** genetic variation between species

24. Which process modifies an organism's genome to introduce a useful characteristic?

- [ ] **A** tissue culture
- [ ] **B** selective breeding
- [ ] **C** asexual reproduction
- [ ] **D** genetic engineering

25. What is the definition of a pathogen?

- [ ] **A** all bacteria
- [ ] **B** all bacteria and viruses
- [ ] **C** any kind of microorganism
- [ ] **D** a disease-causing microorganism

26. How is tuberculosis spread?

....

27. Which of these is a chemical defence of the body?

- [ ] **A** mucus
- [ ] **C** skin
- [ ] **B** lysozyme
- [ ] **D** cilia

28. Which type of disease can be treated with antibiotics?

....

29. What are BMI and waist : hip ratio used to assess?

....

30. Which gas is a product of photosynthesis?

....

31. Which of these factors will not limit the rate of photosynthesis?

- [ ] **A** light intensity
- [ ] **B** carbon dioxide concentration of
- [ ] **C** oxygen concentration of air
- [ ] **D** temperature

32. Which tissue carries dissolved sucrose around a plant?

....

33. What controls phototropism in plants?

- [ ] **A** auxin
- [ ] **B** gibberellin
- [ ] **C** ethene gas
- [ ] **D** gravity

34. How are hormones transported in the human body?

....

35. Where are the sex hormones LH and FSH produced?

- [ ] **A** ovaries
- [ ] **B** testes
- [ ] **C** pituitary
- [ ] **D** thyroid

36. Which gland produces the hormones which control blood glucose concentration?

☐ **A** pancreas   ☐ **B** thyroid

☐ **C** adrenal   ☐ **D** pituitary

37. Which hormone is involved in osmoregulation?

☐ **A** insulin   ☐ **B** glucagon

☐ **C** thyroxine   ☐ **D** ADH

38. In humans, which structure has a large surface area for gas exchange between the air and blood?

....

39. Which component of blood causes blood to clot?

☐ **A** platelets

☐ **B** red blood cells

☐ **C** white blood cells

☐ **D** plasma

40. Which chamber of the heart has the thickest muscular wall and pumps blood to most of the body?

☐ **A** left atrium   ☐ **B** left ventricle

☐ **C** right atrium   ☐ **D** right ventricle

41. What is the product of anaerobic respiration in muscle cells?

....

42. Which of these is a biotic factor of the environment?

☐ **A** light intensity

☐ **B** competition

☐ **C** temperature

☐ **D** water availability

43. Which type of dependent relationship benefits both partner species? 106

....

44. Which trophic level feeds on herbivores? 109

☐ **A** producers

☐ **B** primary consumers

☐ **C** secondary consumers

☐ **D** tertiary consumers

45. Which group of organisms causes decay of dead plants and animals? 113

☐ **A** pathogens

☐ **B** decomposers

☐ **C** parasites

☐ **D** animal vectors

46. Why do farmers add fertilisers to soil where crop plants grow? 115

☐ **A** they contain nutrients that plants need

☐ **B** they prevent damage to crops by pests

☐ **C** they kill fungal pathogens

☐ **D** they kill weed plants

47. Which organism indicates the presence of pollution in water? 116

☐ **A** bloodworm

☐ **B** blackspot fungus

☐ **C** lichen

☐ **D** stonefly

1–6,
15–18,
26–27

Cells, division and growth

What's it all about?

Cells

Prokaryote (bacteria) cells and **eukaryote** (plant and animal) cells can be distinguished by structure. **Microscopes** help us see cell structure more clearly

 Most cells in plants and animals are **specialised** for a particular function, for example:

Animal cells	Plant cells
• egg cell	• root hair cell
• sperm cell	• xylem
• blood cell	• phloem
• ciliated epithelial cell	

 Stem cells are **unspecialised cells** that can divide and differentiate to produce differe types of specialised cell.

Embryonic stem cells come fro embryos; **adult stem cells** com from differentiated tissue.

Each type of stem cell has advantages and disadvantages when used in medical treatment

embryonic stem cells

✓ easy to extract from embryo

✓ produce any type of cell

✗ embryo destroyed when cells removed – some people think embryos have a right to life

all stem cells

✓ replace faulty cell with healthy cell, so person is well again

! stem cells may not stop dividing, and so cause cancer

adult stem cells

✓ no embryo destroyed so not an ethical issue

✓ if taken from the person to be treated, will not cause rejection by the body

✗ produce only a few types of cell

✓ – Advantage   ✗ – Disadvantage   ! – Risk

Growth of babies and young children may be recorded i growth charts.

Cell division

There are two types of cell division: mitosis and meiosis.

	Mitosis	Meiosis
Parent cell	diploid	diploid
Daughter cells	two diploid genetically identical	four (after two divisions) haploid genetically different
Occurs in	• body cells for growth and repair as part of cell cycle • asexual reproduction	• gamete-producing cells • sexual reproduction

Growth

Growth is a permanent increa in size, for examp measured by mas or length. It invo cell division and differentiation in plants and animal In plants, growth also involves cell elongation.

Worked example

mitochondrion measures 0.000 002 m.

a) Write this in standard form. **(1 mark)**

$\times 10^{-6}$ m

Maths skills   Questions about cells may include converting units and using standard form.

b) Write this in micrometres. **(1 mark)**

micrometres or 2 μm

Maths skills   Remember to count the number of decimal places.

Maths skills   Remember that 'micro' means 10^{-6}.

Worked example

Healthy strawberry plants produce new plants from runners as shown in the diagram. Strawberry plants also produce seeds that may be spread far from the parent plant.

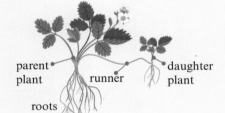

parent plant   runner   daughter plant

roots

Examiner's hint

This question is referring to the two types of reproduction: asexual and sexual. The answer needs to identify when each type of reproduction is beneficial.

Explain the benefit to the strawberry plant of the two types of reproduction. **(4 marks)**

Plants produced from runners are genetically identical to the parent (asexual reproduction). Because the parent is growing well, the daughter plants growing next to it should also grow well.

Plants produced from seeds show genetic variation (sexual reproduction). Conditions far from the parent plant may be different, so genetic variation in the offspring means there is a better chance some of them will grow well in new locations.

Knowledge check

Asexual reproduction produces genetically identical offspring. Sexual reproduction produces offspring that vary genetically.

Examiner's hint

Your answer could also refer to asexual reproduction being faster because there is no need for fertilisation.

Exam practice

1. The diagram shows part of a lily leaf.

   Explain the distribution of
   chloroplasts shown. **(4 marks)**

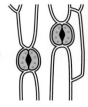

2. Below is a drawing of a plant cell as seen under a
   light microscope using an eyepiece of ×10 and an
   objective lens of ×40.

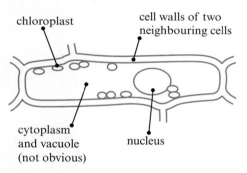

   chloroplast

   cell walls of two
   neighbouring cells

   cytoplasm
   and vacuole
   (not obvious)

   nucleus

   The length of the magnified image of the cell
   is 6.4 cm.

   Calculate the actual size of the plant cell in μm.
   (4 marks)

.... μm

. Multiple sclerosis (MS) is caused by some cells of the immune system damaging nerve cells.

In one medical study, people in the early stages of MS were given drugs to boost growth of stem cells in their bone marrow. The stem cells were extracted, then most of the immune system cells were killed by radiation. Healthy stem cells were placed back in the patient's body to rebuild their immune system. After 3 years, most of the people still showed no symptoms of MS.

Explain the use of the patient's stem cells in this treatment.   **(3 marks)**

Synoptic link

Remember the normal role of the immune system is to destroy any cell that does not belong in the body, for example, pathogens. This can affect transplants of other cells in medical treatments.

. Each month for the first year of a baby boy's life, his mass is plotted on a percentile growth curve. In the first 6 months, his mass lies on the 50th percentile. In the next 6 months, his mass lies above the 75th percentile.

Explain what these measurements show.   **(3 marks)**

Knowledge check

Half of all babies will have a mass equal to or below the 50th percentile curve on a percentile growth chart.

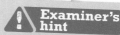

Examiner's hint

One of the marks is for giving a reason for the change in growth rate.

Enzymes in action

What's it all about?

Enzymes catalyse many reactions in living cells, including respiration and photosynthesis. The main types of reaction are:

- **synthesis** – where two or more substrate molecules join to form a larger molecule (for example, when building new cells)
- **breakdown** – when one molecule is broken into smaller molecules (as in digestion of food).

Enzymes are **specific** because only a substrate molecule of the right shape will fit into the enzyme's **active site**.

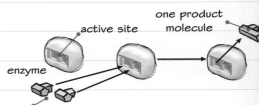

active site   one product molecule

enzyme

two different substrate molecules

Rate of reaction

The rate of an enzyme-catalysed reaction is affected by:

- temperature
- pH
- substrate concentration.

At a given substrate concentration, the fastest rate of an enzyme-controlled reaction happens at the **optimum** (for example, optimum temperature, optimum pH).

Calculating rate

The rate of a reaction is calculated as $\frac{1}{time}$

For example:

if all starch was digested in 20 s

rate of reaction = $\frac{1}{20}$ = 0.05/s

Remember to use the correct units.

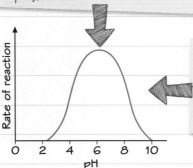

Extreme pH or high temperature permanently deforms the shape of the active site so the enzyme no longer catalyses the reaction – the enzyme is **denatured**.

Worked example

he graph shows the effect of temperature on the rate of an nzyme-controlled reaction.

xplain why the rate of reaction changes as temperature changes.
(4 marks)

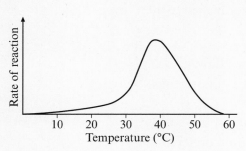

> You are not asked when the reaction stops, so do not refer to denaturation in your answer.

s temperature increases from 0°C up to the optimum, ne rate of reaction increases. This is because the olecules have more kinetic energy, so the substrate olecules are more likely to collide with the enzyme's ctive site and fit into it.

s temperature increases above the optimum, the rate f reaction decreases. This is because the active site ecomes more and more distorted, so it becomes ore difficult for substrate molecules to fit into the ctive site and react.

> This answer is clearly set out to explain why the rate changes, firstly up to the optimum, and then above the optimum.

Worked example

he graph shows the results of xperiments to find out how substrate oncentration affects the rate of an nzyme-controlled reaction.

xplain the shape of the graph at points and B.
(4 marks)

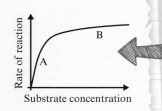

> ⚠ **Examiner's hint**
>
> The command word in this question is 'explain'. This means you need to give a reason for the shape, not simply describe it.

t point A, adding more substrate increases the rate of eaction. This is because some enzyme molecules have mpty active sites, so more substrate molecules can : in them and react.

t point B, all enzyme molecules have a full active site, o adding more substrate has no effect on the rate f reaction.

> This answer is well structured. It explains what happens at point A, and then what happens at point B.

Exam practice

1. The following method was used by students to measure the effect of pH on amylase activity.

- Add $1\,cm^3$ amylase to $2\,cm^3$ starch solution in a tube, buffered at pH 5.
- Place the tube in a beaker of water heated to 40 °C over a Bunsen burner.
- Take a sample of the mixture every 15 s and mix it with a fresh drop of iodine solution in a dimple tile.
- Continue testing until the iodine solution stops changing colour.
- Record the time taken to this point.
- Repeat the method with the solution buffered at pH 6, 7 and 8.

Explain two ways that this method could be improved. **(4 marks)**

Practical skills

Think about the practi
work you have done o
pH and enzyme activit
Is there anything in thi
method that you know
could be done better?

Examiner's hint

If you are asked to criticise a practical method, you should consider:

- safety
- accuracy
- repeatability.

2. Hypothermia occurs when body temperature falls below 35 °C. Symptoms include tiredness and confusion.

Explain these symptoms. **(2 marks)**

Examiner's hint

The question mention
temperature, so use
your knowledge of th
effect of temperature
on cell reactions.

Examiner's hint

Other effects of hypothermia include shivering and pale sk
These are homeostat
responses which are not relevant to this question.

Exam practice

3. Pancreatic juice contains proteases, amylase and substances with a high pH.

Describe the function of pancreatic juice.   **(4 marks)**

> **⚠ Examiner's hint**
>
> Protease enzymes work with proteins and amylase works with starch. Make sure you know which enzyme works with which substrate.

> **💡 Knowledge check**
>
> The pancreas is part of the digestive system. Some pancreatic cells produce the components of digestive juice. Other cells produce the hormones insulin and glucagon.

4. Students investigated the effect of temperature on the rate of starch digestion by amylase. The table shows the time taken for complete digestion of 1.0 g starch at different temperatures.

Temperature (°C)	10	20	30	40	50
Time to complete digestion (s)	1020	580	340	180	960

Calculate the rate of starch digestion at 30 °C. Give your answer in g/s in standard form.   **(2 marks)**

> **⚠ Examiner's hint**
>
> Always show your working in a calculation. You may gain a mark for setting it out correctly, even if you get the answer wrong.

.... g/s

12–13, 75, 93–95

Getting into and out of cells

What's it all about?

Getting into and out of cells

Substances enter and leave cells in three different ways.

 Diffusion is the net movement of molecules down their concentration gradient.

Diffusion is important in living organisms for:

- gas exchange between plant leaves and the air
- absorption of most digested food substances in the small intestine
- gas exchange between air and blood in alveoli in human lungs.

 Osmosis is the net movement of water molecules across a partially permeable membrane (for example, the cell membrane) from the more dilute solution (more water molecules) to the more concentrated solution (fewer water molecules), down its concentration gradient.

Osmosis is important in organisms for:

- the absorption of water by plant root hair cells
- the reabsorption of water in the kidneys.

 In **active transport**, molecules move against their concentration gradient across the cell membrane, using energy from respiration.

Active transport is important in:

- the absorption of mineral ions by plant root hair cells
- the absorption of glucose from food in the small intestine.

Surface area to volume ratio

As size increases, volume increases more rapidly than surface area. This explains why multicellular plants and animals need large exchange surfaces and transport systems.

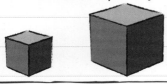

Fick's law

rate of diffusion across a membrane

$$\propto \frac{\text{surface area} \times \text{concentration difference}}{\text{thickness of membrane}}$$

Rate of diffusion increases as surface area and concentration difference increase, and as membrane thickness decreases.

Worked example

The initial mass of a potato slice was 3.54 g. After soaking in a solution, the final mass of the slice was 12.98 g.

Calculate the percentage change in mass. **(4 marks)**

Percentage change in mass

$$= \frac{\text{final mass} - \text{initial mass}}{\text{initial mass}} \times 100$$

$$= \frac{12.98 - 13.54}{13.54} \times 100$$

$$= -4.14\%$$

Maths skills

To calculate percentage change:

1. calculate the difference
2. divide answer to step 1 by the initial mass
3. multiply the answer to step 2 by 100.

It is important to include the minus sign to show that the potato mass decreased during the experiment.

Worked example

Explain how water and mineral ions enter root hair cells in plants. **(4 marks)**

Water molecules enter root hair cells by osmosis because there is net movement of water molecules from the dilute soil solution to the more concentrated cytoplasm.

Mineral ions enter root hair cells by active transport because energy is needed to move the ions against their concentration gradient, from the dilute soil solution to the more concentrated cell cytoplasm.

The solution surrounding root hair cells is usually more dilute than the cytoplasm of the cell, so diffusion won't work for mineral ions.

This answer clearly sets out what happens for water and then for mineral ions. In each case, it provides a reason for the named method of movement.

Exam practice

1. A potato strip of mass 14.26 g was placed in a $0.6 \, mol/dm^3$ sucrose solution. After 20 minutes, the mass of the potato strip was measured as 11.71 g.

   Calculate the percentage change in mass of the potato strip, to 2 d.p. **(2 marks)**

Examiner's hint

Always show your working. You may gain a mark for setting out the calculation correct even if you get the wrong answer.

Examiner's hint

Make sure your answer is in the form asked for in the question.
Your answer should include + for percentage gain or − for percentage loss.

2. The diagram shows a single alveolus and its capillary.

   Explain the role of breathing and blood flow in gas exchange. **(6 marks)**

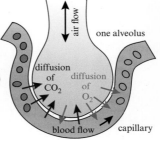

Fick's law tells you that the rate of diffusion is proportional to the concentration difference. This means that if one doubles, th other doubles.

Examiner's hint

Remember, your answe needs to show you hav good knowledge and understanding of the scientific ideas involved You must also present these ideas clearly and in a logical structure.

Please continue your answer on a separate piece of paper if necessary.

xam practice

3. The illustration shows the dimensions of a free-living flatworm.

Key
length 5 mm
width 1 mm
thickness 0.4 mm

(a) Assuming a cuboid shape, calculate the SA : V ratio of the flatworm. **(2 marks)**

Knowledge check

You will need to calculate SA (surface area) and V (volume) and use these to calculate $\frac{SA}{V}$.

....

(b) Use the idea of SA : V ratio to explain why the flatworm has no specialised respiratory surface or transport system. **(3 marks)**

Use the relationship described in Fick's law between surface area and the thickness of the worm to answer this question.

4. Explain why leaf stomata open during the day and close at night. **(4 marks)**

Synoptic link

Your answer will need to describe how stomata affect the rate of photosynthesis and transpiration.

19–24

The nervous system

What's it all about?

Neurones

- **Nerve cells** include sensory neurones, relay neurones (in the CNS) and motor neurones.
- **Adaptations** of neurones include long axons, many terminals and myelin for insulation.

Problems in the brain and spinal cord

Diagnosis

CT and PET scanning help us to see the brain inside the skull. CT scanning shows tissues (including tumours).
PET scanning shows brain function.

Treatment

Spinal injuries are difficult to treat because there are no stem cells in nerve tissue.

Brain tumours may require surgery to open the skull, or drugs that cross the blood–brain barrier.

Synapses

The gap where two or more neurones meet is called a synapse.
One neurone may connect to several others.

I Electrical impulse reaches the axon terminal of first neurone

2 Impulse triggers release of chemical neurotransmitter into the synaptic gap

synapse

3 Neurotransmitter diffuses across the gap, triggering an electrical impulse in the next neurone

Synapses ensure nerve impulses only travel in one direction.

The eye

- The cornea and lens focus light rays.
- The iris controls the size of the pupil.
- The rod and cone cells of the retina respond to light.

Eye problem	Treatment
short-sightedness: light rays focus before retina	diverging lens
long-sightedness: light rays focus behind retina	converging lens
cataract: clouding of the lens	lens replaced with clear plastic one

Reflex responses

Reflex responses are rapid and always the same because the **reflex arc** is short and the brain (conscious thought) is not involved.

18

Worked example

xplain why a person with cataracts
an see more clearly after a
ataract operation.   **(3 marks)**

 cataract is a clouding of the
ens. This reduces the amount of
ght that reaches the retina so the
mage is not clear. In a cataract
peration, the cloudy lens is
eplaced with a clear plastic lens
o more light can reach the retina
nd a clearer image is formed.

This answer is good because it begins
by describing what a cataract is.
This makes it clear how the operation
improves vision.

Note that replacing the lens
could also help to solve problems
with long- or short-sightedness.
However, because the plastic lens
cannot change shape, spectacles are
still needed for seeing clearly at the
opposite end of the visual range.

Worked example

Multiple sclerosis is caused by the
radual loss of myelin from nerve cells.

Explain why some people with multiple
clerosis have difficulty walking.
          (3 marks)

Myelin surrounds nerve cells,
nsulating them from other cells
nd allowing nerve impulses to
ass quickly along the axon.
Damage to the myelin will slow
he nerve impulses and may allow
mpulses to jump from one axon
o another, so they do not get
o where they are meant to go.
 nerve impulses to leg muscles
re disrupted, then the person will
ave difficulty walking.

A good start to this answer is to
describe the function of myelin in
healthy nerve cells. This makes it
easier to explain clearly why damage
to the myelin causes problems
with walking.

Exam practice

1. When you move from a dark room into a bright area, your pupil immediately reduces in size.

   Explain how the reflex that controls this response helps to protect the eye. **(3 marks)**

Knowledge check

Describing the reflex in your answer will hel you to explain what is important in this respo

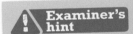

Examiner's hint

The question has three marks, so make sure y include three separate points in your answer.

2. Explain the function of synapses in the nervous system. **(3 marks)**

Examiner's hint

As with many 'explain' questions, you should start your answer by describing, before explaining.

Knowledge check

Remember that chemic neurotransmitter molecules are only released from one neurone into the synaptic gap. Also think about the structure of neurones.

am practice

. In Alzheimer's disease, clumps of toxic amyloid proteins build up in the brain. This causes brain cells to die, leading to memory loss. In the early 2000s, scientists developed a radioactive substance that attaches to amyloid.

Doctors need a way to determine whether someone has early symptoms of Alzheimer's disease.

Describe how the development of this radioactive substance could be used to do this.   **(3 marks)**

> **⚠ Examiner's hint**
>
> This is a 'describe' question, so do not include any reasons in your answer.

> **💡 Knowledge check**
>
> Think about the different ways in which we can look at the brain. Which is most suitable here?

4. Explain how a person's long-sightedness can be corrected.   **(2 marks)**

> **⚠ Examiner's hint**
>
> Start by describing how long-sightedness is caused, then explain how to correct it. The answer needs more than simply 'spectacles' or 'contact lenses': you need to say what type of spectacles or contact lenses and explain what they will do.

21

28–29

DNA and protein synthesis

What's it all about?

DNA structure

- DNA is genetic material formed from two strands of nucleotides coiled round each other to form a double helix.
- Bases on opposite DNA strands are **complementary** (they always form the same base pairs: A with T, C with G).
- Base pairs are linked by weak hydrogen bonds. All those bonds hold the two strands together tightly.
- Coding DNA contains the information needed to produce specific proteins.
- Non-coding DNA includes binding sites for RNA polymerase enzymes.

A nucleotide
P phosphate
base
can be A
G or T
deoxyribose sugar

Protein synthesis

Protein synthesis involves two separate stages:

> To **transcribe** is to copy. (DNA bases are copied into mRNA bases.)

1   **Transcription** is the formation of a complementary mRNA strand for the codir DNA of a gene.

| RNA polymerase enzyme binds to non-coding DNA just before a gene | → | RNA polymerase separates the DNA strands and moves along the DNA | → | RNA polymerase joins together bases complementary to the coding DNA of a gene, forming a complementary mRNA strand |

2   **Translation**

> To **translate** is like changing to another language (from mRNA base sequence on DNA to amino acid sequence in a protein or polypeptide).

(4) Amino acids are joined to make an amino acid chain (a **polypeptide**).   amino acids

(5) tRNA free to collect another amino acid.

(2) tRNA molecules bring amir acids to the ribosome. The a acid attached to each tRNA molecule depends on the orde of bases in the tRNA.

C U A

C C G

C G A A U U
G A U G C U U A A G G C

mRNA strand

(3) Complementary bases of tRNA pair with the bases on the mRNA strand.

(1) The mRNA attaches to a ribosome. Ribosome moves along the mRNA in this direction reading one **triplet of bases** (codon) at a time.

Mutations

A mutation in coding DNA may affect the protein produced.

> A mutation is a change in DNA.

A mutation in non-coding DNA may change the binding of RNA polymerase and alter the amount of protein produced (either increase or decrease).

orked example

ormal haemoglobin forms a blobby shape. Sickle cell
aemoglobin can form a long spiky shape. The change in
ckle cell haemoglobin is caused by the replacement of a
ngle T base by an A base in the β-globin gene that codes
r part of the molecule.

◄ Make sure you
know which stage is
transcription and which
is translation.

.) Explain how a single base change in DNA can cause
this change in shape of a polypeptide. **(4 marks)**

he changed base will form a different
omplementary pair during transcription, so the
RNA strand will have a different base than usual.
uring translation, the codon with the different base
ill join to a different tRNA which carries a different
mino acid. So, the amino acid chain formed from the
ckle cell version of the gene will have one different
mino acid than usual. This amino acid change will
ter the way the chain folds up into a polypeptide
o it will make a different shape.

◄ This answer clearly
sets out the process
from transcription to
translation, and explains
how the mutation
causes changes at
each stage.

orked example

>) β-thalassaemia is caused by a mutation in non-coding
DNA just before the β-globin gene.

Explain how this mutation can result in less β-globin
polypeptide being made than usual. **(2 marks)**

◄ This question requires
understanding of
the role of RNA
polymerase binding in
DNA transcription.

he mutation is in the binding site for the RNA
olymerase just before the gene. If the polymerase
nzyme cannot bind well to the DNA, less DNA is
ranscribed so less protein can be made.

Had a go ☐   Nearly there ☐   Nailed it! ☐

Exam practice

1. A section of the gene that codes for a polypeptide found in haemoglobin has the following DNA sequence:

   TACCTCGTAGAC

   Which sequence shows the complementary DNA strand? **(1 mark)**

   ☐ **A** ATCCTGCAACTG

   ☐ **B** CGTTCTACGAGT

   ☐ **C** ATGGAGCATCTG

   ☐ **D** TTGGTGCATCTG

2. One of the drugs used to treat an HIV infection prevents DNA from the HIV virus inserting into human DNA.

   Explain how this drug can help to reduce the number of HIV viruses in an infected person. **(3 marks)**

Knowledge check

Remember that DNA bases always pair in the same way (A with T, G with C).

Synoptic link

You will need to expla how HIV viruses replicate to answer this question well.

3. The Human Genome Project mapped all the bases in the human genome. Scientists then worked out which sequence of bases formed each gene.

Explain how scientists could use the amino acids in a protein to identify a particular gene.   **(4 marks)**

Examiner's hint

Do not waste time by referring to the Human Genome Project in your answer. Look for the command word in the question. Here, you just need to explain the link between amino acids and genes.

4. PKU is a disease caused by a mutation in a gene that codes for PAH, a liver enzyme. The PAH enzyme breaks down phenylalanine, which is harmful at a high concentration.

Explain how a mutation in the PAH gene could affect the activity of PAH enzyme.   **(3 marks)**

Synoptic link

Use your knowledge of how the shape of an active site affects an enzyme's activity.

Genetics and variation

What's it all about?

Mendel

Mendel studied inheritance in pea plants. The phenotypes he chose were inherited independently of other traits (genes were not known in Mendel's time).

We now know that these traits show **monohybrid** inheritance (characteristics controlled by a single gene).

We now know that phenotypes which 'disappear' in a generation are controlled by a **recessive** allele, which only affects the phenotype when the **dominant** allele for that gene is not present.

Mendel found that:

- a cross between **pure-breeding** parents with different phenotypes (for example, tall × dwarf plants) produces offspring that all have the same phenotype (tall)

- crossing the offspring produces a **3 : 1 ratio** of the phenotype seen in the first-generation offspring compared with the other parental phenotype (3 tall : 1 dwarf).

Key terminology

genotype – the alleles for a particular gene or characteristic

phenotype – the characteristics of an organism

homozygous – having two identical alleles for a gene

heterozygous – having two different alleles for a gene

Inheritance diagrams

Genetic diagram   Punnett square   Family pedigree

Genetic diagrams and **Punnet squares** show possible offspring. **Family pedigree** show actual offspring.

Sex-linked inheritance

Where an X chromosome has the **recessive** allele for a gene:

recessive allele

dominant allele

X Y   X X
male   female

- males will develop the phenotype if that gene is missing on the Y chromosome

- females who are heterozygous will not develop the phenotype – they are **carriers** for the recessive phenotype.

Codominance

Codominance occurs when both alleles in a heterozygous individual are expressed equally in the phenotype, for example, in people who have the blood group AB.

Human Genome Project

Studying the human genome shows many genetic differences between individuals, some of which have implications for disorders and their medical treatment.

Worked example

The ability to taste phenylthiocarbamide (PTC) is a dominant condition. The diagram shows the inheritance of PTC tasting in one family.

Describe the evidence that PTC tasting is controlled by a dominant allele. **(2 marks)**

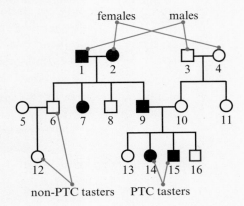

You are asked for evidence, so make sure you refer to specific individuals in the pedigree.

1 and 2 are both PTC tasters but they have two children who are non-tasters. Therefore, PTC tasting must be dominant and non-tasting must be recessive.

Worked example

Describe two possible developments as a result of decoding the human genome, and discuss the implications of these developments. **(4 marks)**

One development is the identification of genes that can cause disease. Knowing if a person has a faulty gene could help that person and their family to prepare for its effects, but some people would prefer not to know if they have a faulty gene, because it might make them worry about it.

Another development is gene therapy. This involves replacing faulty alleles in body cells with healthy ones. This allows the affected person to live a normal life. However, people will have to decide whether the faulty alleles are replaced in gametes, so that the healthy alleles can be passed on to children.

There are many possible answers to this question, because there are many new developments. Other possibilities include: creating personalised medicines and identifying evolutionary relationships between humans and other organisms. As well as learning about new developments, you need to be able to say what the implications are.

Exam practice

1. A man and a woman are heterozygous for the gene that controls ABO blood group. The man has the phenotype group A and the woman has the phenotype group B.

   Draw a Punnett square to calculate the probability of the couple having a child with the phenotype blood group AB. **(4 marks)**

⚠ Examiner's hint

Make sure you define the alleles you use in your answer, so it is clear what you mean. You could use I^A for the allele that produces the A phenotype, I^B for the allele that produce the B phenotype, and for the allele that produc the O phenotype.

💡 Knowledge check

Remember that the A and B alleles for the ABO blood group gene show codominance, whi the O allele is recessive to both A and B.

2. Red-green colour blindness is a recessive, sex-linked disorder. The diagram shows the phenotypes of individuals in a family for this characteristic.

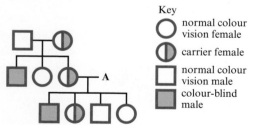

Key
⚪ normal colour vision female
◑ carrier female
☐ normal colour vision male
⬛ colour-blind male

   State and explain the phenotype of person A. **(3 marks)**

⚠ Examiner's hint

Make sure you interpr the family pedigree correctly using the information given. Note here that the disorder is sex-linked well as being caused a recessive allele.

⚠ Examiner's hint

It may help to write on the diagram the genoty of key individuals that c help you to answer the question. Start by work out the genotype of A's partner and children.

3. The table shows the results of one of Mendel's experiments with pea plants. The first-generation offspring were produced by crossing plants of the yellow seed phenotype with plants of the green seed phenotype. The second-generation offspring were produced by crossing first-generation offspring with each other.

Examiner's hint

A 'discuss' question expects an answer that investigates the situation using reasoning or argument.

Parent phenotypes	Yellow seeds	Green seeds
first-generation offspring phenotypes	6854	0
second-generation offspring phenotypes	6022	2001

Maths skills

It will help to calculate the ratio of phenotypes in the second-generation offspring.

Discuss how these results led Mendel to propose a hypothesis that offspring inherit discrete 'particles' (now known as genes) from their parents. **(4 marks)**

4. In a particular plant, yellow flowers are dominant to white flowers. A plant breeder has a plant that produces yellow flowers.

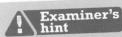

Examiner's hint

Using Punnett squares will help you to present your answer clearly.

Explain why a test cross of this plant with a white-flower plant will show if this plant is homozygous or heterozygous. **(4 marks)**

REVISION GUIDE 39–41

Evolution and classification

What's it all about?

Evolution through natural selection

Darwin and Wallace separately used the idea of **natural selection** to explain how species change over time (**evolution**).

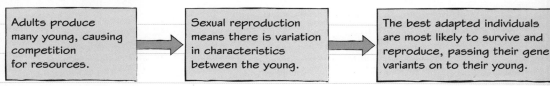

| Adults produce many young, causing competition for resources. | → | Sexual reproduction means there is variation in characteristics between the young. | → | The best adapted individuals are most likely to survive and reproduce, passing their gene variants on to their young. |

This theory interprets similarities and differences in characteristics and DNA between organisms to decide how closely related organisms are, such as in the evolution of the **pentadactyl limb** of vertebrates.

Evolution of resistance

Evolution of resistance (for example, antibiotic resistance in bacteria) can be explained by the theory of evolution by natural selection.

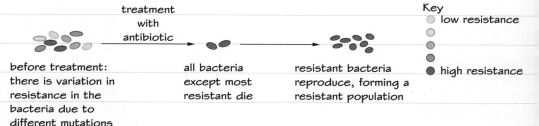

before treatment: there is variation in resistance in the bacteria due to different mutations

all bacteria except most resistant die

resistant bacteria reproduce, forming a resistant population

Key
○ low resistance
○
○
●
● high resistance

Human evolution

Evidence for human evolution can be found in:

- fossils of human skeletons
- stone tools dated from the sediments in which they were found.

Changes in classification

The five **kingdoms** (animals, plants, fungi, protists, prokaryotes) are now classified as three **domains** (Bacteria, Archaea, Eukarya).

The change results from the discovery of single-celled bacteria-like organisms that have some different genes from those in bacteria. These genes code for a different ribosome structure and some different proteins.

Worked example

The diagram shows the bones of the forelimbs of two living vertebrates.

Explain how the limbs provide evidence for Darwin's theory of evolution. **(3 marks)**

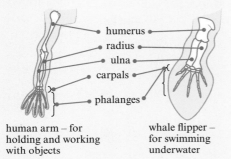

human arm – for holding and working with objects

whale flipper – for swimming underwater

The limbs have the same basic structure of one long upper bone, two long lower bones, several carpals and five phalanges. This suggests that they evolved from the same common ancestor. The limbs have evolved in different ways owing to natural selection, making them better adapted for different purposes.

Many living vertebrates have the same **pentadactyl** (five-fingered) limb structure.

This answer clearly describes the similarities in the diagrams which you would expect to see in organisms that have evolved from a common ancestor. The answer then links to natural selection, which is part of Darwin's theory.

Worked example

The diagram shows the three-domain system of classification defined by Carl Woese (1928–2012), which indicates that Archaea are more closely related to Eukarya than to Bacteria. Before Carl Woese suggested this system, organisms in the Bacteria and Archaea domains were classified together as Prokaryotes.

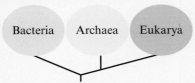

Bacteria   Archaea   Eukarya

Explain this change in classification. **(2 marks)**

Archaea organisms have many similar characteristics to Bacteria, which is why they were grouped together. However, analysis of their genes and chemistry has provided evidence that they are more different from bacteria than all other organisms, and so should be classified in a separate group.

The diagram is a **phylogenetic tree**, with nodes that represent extinct common ancestors. Groups that are more closely related have a more recent common ancestor.

This answer gives two very separate points, one for each mark.

Exam practice

1. In the 1940s, doctors began treating infections caused by the bacterium *Staphylococcus aureus* ('staph') with the antibiotic penicillin. Less than 10 years later, penicillin-resistant staph bacteria had evolved.

   Explain how this example provides evidence for the theory of evolution by natural selection. **(3 marks)**

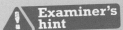

Examiner's hint
You need to explain the evolution of resistance in bacteria in this question. The question is not about immunity to infection.

2. Moles are small mammals that dig tunnels to catch earthworms to eat. The illustrations show the Eastern mole of North America and the European mole.

Eastern mole   European mole

   Analysis of their skeletons suggests they are closely related, but DNA analysis shows they are only distantly related.

   Explain why DNA analysis is considered more accurate in identifying evolutionary relationships. **(3 marks)**

Examiner's hint
There are three things to cover in your answer.
Explain why:
- the skeletons are similar
- the DNA is not similar
- DNA analysis is better.

am practice

3. Jean-Baptiste Lamarck (1744–1829) produced a theory of evolution due to acquired characteristics. The flowchart shows how Lamarck explained the evolution of long necks in giraffes.

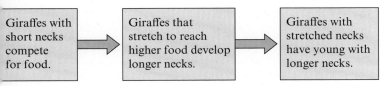

| Giraffes with short necks compete for food. | → | Giraffes that stretch to reach higher food develop longer necks. | → | Giraffes with stretched necks have young with longer necks. |

Compare and contrast Lamarck's theory of evolution and Darwin's theory of evolution. **(4 marks)**

> **⚠ Examiner's hint**
>
> 'Compare and contrast' questions require you to look for at least one similarity and one difference between two or more things. You do not need to draw a conclusion from the comparison.

> **💡 Knowledge check**
>
> Remember that Darwin's theory describes how species change because of natural selection and inheritance of better-adapted characteristics.

4. The fossil 'Lucy' has been classified as *Australopithecus afarensis*. Other fossils of this species have been found in several parts of East Africa. Some scientists think that Lucy's species are direct ancestors of *Homo habilis*, which lived 1.6 million years ago in East Africa.

Explain why it is difficult to be certain that *Australopithecus afarensis* is the direct ancestor of *Homo habilis*. **(2 marks)**

> **⚠ Examiner's hint**
>
> There are several possible answers to this question. Think about:
> - when the two species lived
> - the effect of not all dead organisms forming fossils
> - the fact that classification of these species depends only on evidence from fossil bones.

42–47

Genetic engineering and selective breeding

What's it all about?

Genetic engineering and selective breeding are used to improve useful characteristics in organisms.

	Genetic engineering	Selective breeding
Description	Genetic engineering involves altering the genome of an organism, usually by adding a gene for a useful characteristic from another species.	Animals and plants are selectively bred to improve useful characteristics.
Examples	• bacteria, yeast or mammals that produce medicines for humans • crop plants resistant to pests or herbicides	• to increase yields of milk or meat • to increase grain yields
Benefits	👍 rapid production from bacteria or yeast 👍 increased yield of crop plants	👍 more food for us
Risks	👎 transfer of the gene to other organisms in the environment, which can impact on environmental relationships (e.g. food, shelter) with other species	👎 damage to health of animals that are too heavy or produce too much milk 👎 reduced genetic diversity which increases health risks to the animals

Tissue culture

Tissue culture is the growing of new tissue from cells. This uses mitosis, so the cells produced are genetically identical. Tissue culture of:

- human cells is used in the testing of new medicines
- plant cells produces whole plants that are genetically identical (**asexual reproduction**), which is useful for producing genetically-engineered plants.

Increasing food production

Other ways to produce more food include

- **fertilisers** – adding nutrients to soil to increase crop growth (see pages 62–65)
- **biological control** – using organisms (predators or parasites) to control pests.

Worked example

People with haemophilia are unable to make a protein that causes blood to clot. The disorder used to be treated by giving patients clotting protein extracted from human blood. Now bacteria have been genetically engineered to make the protein.

'Discuss' questions require an answer that explores all aspects of an issue, including benefits and risks.

Discuss the possible benefits and risks of making clotting proteins using modified bacteria rather than extracting them from blood. **(3 marks)**

Using bacteria makes it possible to produce the clotting proteins more quickly than extracting them from blood, because bacteria reproduce quickly. It also avoids the risk of transferring viruses or other pathogens from infected blood. One risk of using modified bacteria is that the proteins may not work as well as those from blood, because they may be slightly different.

This answer contains two benefits and one risk for the 3 marks. Alternative benefits include:
- bacteria are grown in a fermenter so production is not dependent on the availability of blood
- it is easier to produce larger quantities of proteins.

Alternative risks include:
- concerns about GM organisms entering the environment
- the bacteria entering people who do not need the protein.

Worked example

Red spider mite is a pest of greenhouse crops. A predatory mite that feeds on the pest can be used as a biological control.

Explain the advantages and disadvantages of this. **(3 marks)**

Synoptic link

This answer effectively uses knowledge of feeding relationships and how they affect predator and prey numbers.

The predatory mite feeds on the red spider mite, so it gets rid of the pest but not other useful insects. The red spider mite cannot develop resistance to it, and the predatory mite only needs to be introduced once because it reproduces in the greenhouse. A disadvantage is that it does not get rid of the red spider mite completely. When the red spider mite population falls, the predatory mite runs out of food so its population falls as well.

Exam practice

1. Maize (sweetcorn) has been genetically modified to produce a bacterial toxin that kills corn rootworms. Corn rootworm is a major pest of maize crops.
   The chart shows the results of many studies on the impact of genetically-modified maize on yield and rootworms.

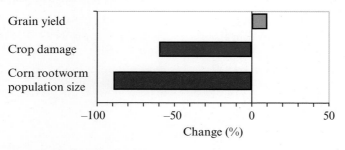

> **⚠ Examiner's hint**
>
> Read the question carefully. Your answer only needs to explain what is seen in the chart, not other aspec of genetic engineering

Explain the relationship between the changes seen in the chart.   **(3 marks)**

2. Artemisinin is used in drugs to treat people infected with the protist that causes malaria. Artemisinin is extracted from artemisia plants in very small amounts, making the substance expensive. Scientists have genetically engineered artemisia plants to produce more artemisinin.
   Tissue culture is then used to produce new plants.

   Describe three benefits of using tissue culture to make artemisinin.   **(3 marks)**

>  **Synoptic link**
>
> To answer this questio well, use your knowled of mitosis and asexual reproduction.

am practice

. The charts compare how selective breeding has affected the weight gain of chickens reared for meat, and the use of chicken food, between 1960 and 2000.

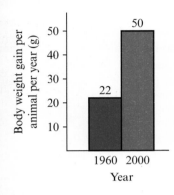 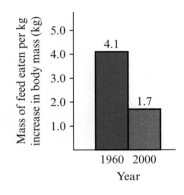

Discuss the benefits and risks of selective breeding of chickens for human food using information from the charts. **(6 marks)**

. Caterpillars can damage crops by eating parts of the plants. The caterpillars can be killed by chemical insecticides. They can also be controlled by biological control using *Trichogramma* wasps which parasitise and kill the caterpillars.

Compare the benefits and risks of each type of control for protecting a crop. **(4 marks)**

49–66

Health, disease and medicine

What's it all about?

There are two types of disease:

1 **Communicable** (infectious) diseases are passed from an infected individual to others, and are caused by pathogens.

Having one disease can increase the risk of developing others, for example, by damaging the immune system.

2 **Non-communicable** diseases cannot be passed directly from someone with the disease to others (except some via genes)

Obesity is a risk factor for many non-communicable diseases.
Obesity can be measured using body mass index (BMI) or waist : hip ratio.

Viruses

Viruses cause many diseases. Some viruses have two pathways in their life cycle:

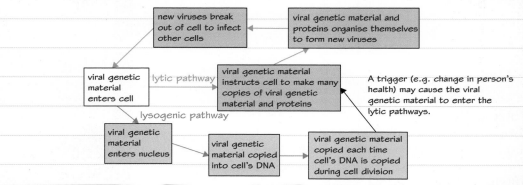

Key health terms

- **Antibiotics** treat bacterial infections by damaging bacterial cell processes but not human cell processes.

- **Immunisation** stimulates the body's immune system to produce antibodies using vaccine containing antigens from the pathogen.

- **Herd immunity** occurs when most people in a population are immune to a disease (through immunisation). This reduces the risk of infection for those who are not immune

- **Monoclonal antibodies** are identical antibodies for the same antigen, produced from hybridoma cells. Hybridoma cells are made by fusing antibody-producing mouse lymphocytes with tumour cells.

38

Worked example

n 2011, there were 15 699 new cases of lung cancer in women in England. In 2015, the number of new cases f lung cancer in this group was 17 620.

Calculate the percentage change in new cases to 1 d.p.

(2 marks)

$$\% \text{ change} = \frac{\text{final value} - \text{initial value}}{\text{initial value}} \times 100$$

$$= \frac{17\,620 - 15\,699}{15\,699} \times 100$$

$$= +12.2\%$$

Maths skills

Always show your working in calculations. You may get a mark for setting out the calculation correctly even if you get the wrong answer.

Worked example

A farmer notices that the crop plants in one part of a field are much shorter than the rest. The whole field was planted with seed at the same time.

Suggest an explanation as to how the farmer could try o identify the cause of the poor growth. **(6 marks)**

Poor growth may be caused by conditions that reduce how much photosynthesis takes place, such as lack of water, light or nutrients in the soil. The farmer could test for these conditions in the field, for example, by using a soil moisture meter or a soil nitrogen test, or by looking to see where there is most shade from nearby trees.

Poor growth can also be caused by pests that eat the plants, such as caterpillars. The farmer can check for this by looking carefully at the plants. Pathogens that infect the plant can also reduce growth by killing cells. These can be difficult to identify in the field. The farmer could get more accurate tests done by sending plant and soil samples to a lab for analysis.

Examiner's hint

Start by identifying the main points you need to include, then organise them into a logical sequence before you write.

Examiner's hint

This is a good answer because it includes relevant scientific knowledge and is clearly presented.

Answers for 6 mark questions are marked as follows:
1–2 marks for some scientific ideas and explanations.
3–4 marks for structured explanations and good range of scientific knowledge.
5–6 marks for a well-structured, coherent and logical answer with detailed accurate and relevant scientific knowledge.

39

Had a go ☐   Nearly there ☐   Nailed it! ☐

Exam practice

1. Explain how monoclonal antibodies are produced to kill cancer cells. **(4 marks)**

2. Two men have the same BMI and are classed as overweight. Man A has a waist measurement of 102 cm and a hip measurement of 101 cm. Man B has a waist measurement of 96 cm and a hip measurement of 104 cm.

   Discuss the risks of each man dying from cardiovascular disease. **(3 marks)**

xam practice

3. The effect of antibiotics on bacterial growth can be tested by placing discs containing the antibiotic on a bacterial lawn plate.

   Describe three ways in which aseptic technique is used in this experiment. **(3 marks)**

Practical skills

Use your knowledge from the Core Practical that investigates the effect of antiseptics, antibiotics or plant extracts on microbial cultures to answer this question. What did you do to minimise the chance of infection of the culture by microorganisms in the air or on the equipment?

4. Measles is an infectious disease spread in droplets from coughs and sneezes. Most UK babies are immunised against measles. Some babies cannot be immunised because their immune system is too weak.

   Explain why these individuals are protected against measles if most other people have been immunised. **(2 marks)**

Knowledge check

Herd immunity is where the few non-immunised people in a population are protected from infection because everyone else is immunised.

5. Two plant extracts were tested for their antibacterial properties against a particular species of bacterium. Filter paper discs dipped in the extracts were placed on an agar plate inoculated with bacteria.

   Describe how you would tell which plant extract was better at killing the bacteria. **(1 mark)**

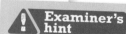
Examiner's hint

There is only one mark for this answer, so do not spend time adding more detail than is needed.

68–76

Photosynthesis and transport

What's it all about?

Adaptations of a leaf for photosynthesis include the following:

1 Chloroplasts which are mostly in the palisade cells near the upper surface of the leaf.

 2 Stomata in the lower surface of the leaf through which gases are exchanged with the environment by diffusion.

 3 Large air spaces in the leaf which provide a large surface area for diffusion into and out of cells.

Limiting factors

Temperature, carbon dioxide concentration and light intensity are all **limiting factors** for the rate of photosynthesis.

Transpiration

Transpiration is the flow of water through a plant in **xylem**. Water flows from the roots to the leaves, where it evaporates into the air through stomata. Dissolved minerals are carried in the water through the plant.

Xylem vessels are long empty tubes made from dead cells, through which water flows easily. The vessels have thick lignified walls to prevent stretching or collapse.

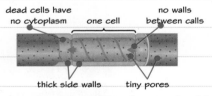

dead cells have no cytoplasm   one cell   no walls between cells

thick side walls   tiny pores

The rate of evaporation from a leaf is affected by:

- temperature (due to the kinetic energy of molecules)
- wind speed (due to concentration gradients)
- light intensity (because stomata close as light intensity decreases).

Inverse square law

Light intensity is inversely proportional to the square of the distance from a light source:

$$\text{light intensity} \propto \frac{1}{d^2}$$

When light is the limiting factor, the rate of photosynthesis is inversely proportional to $\frac{1}{d^2}$.

Translocation

Translocation is the flow of dissolved sucrose produced from glucose after photosynthesis. It moves through **phloem** from leaves to other parts of the plant.

The end walls of phloem cells (sieve plates) have holes that allow fluid to pass through easily. Phloem includes living cells that pump sucrose into and out of the transport cells.

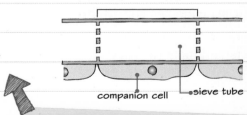

companion cell   sieve tube

Translocation can be in any direction. Transpiration is in one direction only.

Worked example

Explain the relationship between rate of photosynthesis and temperature shown in the graph.
(4 marks)

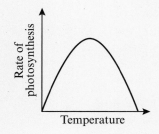

The **optimum** temperature is where the rate is at its highest (the peak).

Rate of photosynthesis increases as temperature increases. This is because the molecules are moving faster, so they collide more often and with more energy; this means reactions happen more often.

Remember that temperature affects the kinetic energy of molecules. This is shown by the rising part of the graph line.

Rate of photosynthesis decreases as temperature increases beyond the optimum, because the enzymes that control the reactions are becoming denatured and the substrate cannot fit into the active site so well.

Remember that most reactions in cells (including those of photosynthesis) are controlled by enzymes, which are affected by temperature.

Worked example

The diagram shows two guard cells surrounding a stoma.

Explain the role of chloroplasts and osmosis in the opening of stomata in daylight.
(3 marks)

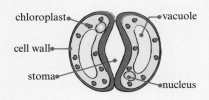

chloroplast · · vacuole

cell wall ·

stoma · · nucleus

Guard cells have a thickened cell wall on the inside of the stoma, which cannot stretch as much as the other side.

Chloroplasts produce sugar from photosynthesis when there is enough light. This increases the solute concentration inside the guard cells, so water enters the cells by osmosis. As the outer side of the cell wall stretches more than the part around the stoma, the guard cells distort as more water enters them, opening the stoma.

You could also describe this in terms of decreasing water concentration inside the cell as more glucose is produced.

43

Exam practice

1. Students used the following method to investigate the effect of distance from a light source on the rate of photosynthesis in algae.

   A. Place 20 algal balls in indicator solution in each of three screw-top bottles.

   B. Place each bottle at a different distance from a lamp.

   C. Switch on the lamp for 2 hours.

   D. Then use a pH scale to identify the pH of the solution in each bottle.

   Explain how the method could be improved to give better results. **(6 marks)**

Use your knowledge c the Core Practical wor you did on the effect of light intensity on the rate of photosynthesis to help you identify the weaknesses in this method.

Remember that accura and repeatability are important when designing an experime

Please continue your answer on a separate piece of paper.

2. In a different experiment on the effect of light intensity on the rate of photosynthesis, students measured the number of bubbles of oxygen released by a pondweed plant in a beaker of water at different distances from a lamp.

   At 15 cm from the lamp, the pondweed released 60 bubbles in one minute.

   Calculate the number of bubbles you would expect to be released in one minute when the beaker was 30 cm from the lamp. **(2 marks)**

You will need to use th inverse square law relationship between light intensity and distance: intensity $\propto \frac{1}{d}$
For d, use the fact that the distance has doubled rather than absolute value of 30

xam practice

3. Students were investigating the effect of wind speed on the loss of water from a plant's leaves. They watered a potted plant and weighed it. They then placed the plant in front of a fan on medium speed for 24 hours, after which they weighed the plant again.

   Describe a suitable control for this experiment. **(2 marks)**

Knowledge check

Remember that a control is a copy of the experiment with only one factor changed. All the controlled variables should be the same between the experiment and the control.

4. The graph shows the mean rate of growth of tomato plants grown in different conditions in a glasshouse.

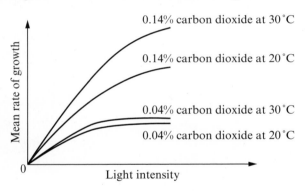

Knowledge check

Light intensity, carbon dioxide concentration and temperature are all limiting factors for the rate of photosynthesis.

Use information from the graph to explain the effect of carbon dioxide and temperature on plant growth. **(4 marks)**

Examiner's hint

Be clear about which pair of lines on the graph you are comparing in each part of your explanation.

Examiner's hint

Note that this question does not ask about light intensity, so do not spend time describing its effect in your answer.

77–78, 80–84

Hormones in animals and plants

What's it all about?

Animal hormones

In animals, hormones are substances released from **endocrine glands** into the blood which affect **target organs** by changing what they are doing.

Menstrual cycle hormones	Produced by	Effects
oestrogen	cells in maturing egg follicles	• stimulates thickening of uterus wall before ovulatio • high concentration triggers surge in LH release • after ovulation maintains uterus wall together with progesterone
progesterone	corpus luteum	• stimulates further thickening of the uterus linir after ovulation • high concentration inhibits release of FSH
FSH	pituitary	• stimulates egg maturation in ovary • stimulates release of oestrogen
LH	pituitary	• high concentration triggers ovulation

Oestrogen and progesterone can be used in hormonal contraception.

Clomifene is used in assisted reproductive technology to stimulate release of FSH and

Thyroxine

Thyroxine affects metabolic rate. It is controlled by negative feedback, via TRH released from the hypothalamus and TSH released from the pituitary to keep its blood concentration within limits.

Adrenalin

Adrenalin prepares the body for action b

• increasing heart rate, blood pressure and blood flow to muscles

• stimulating breakdown of glycogen in the liver to glucose, which is release into the blood.

Plant hormones

Auxins are plant hormones that cause **phototropism** (growth changes in response to light) and **gravitropism** (growth changes in response to gravity). Plant hormone are used commercially to:

• control plant growth
• change growth rates

• stimulate germination
• control flower/fruit formation

• produce seedless fruit
• encourage fruit ripening.

Worked example

Explain, in terms of hormones and their actions, how the progesterone-only pill acts as a contraception.   **(4 marks)**

Progesterone inhibits the release of FSH from the pituitary gland. FSH is needed to stimulate the maturation of an egg in the ovary. A maturing egg would stimulate the release of increasing amounts of oestrogen. Without increasing oestrogen, there is no surge in LH release and therefore no ovulation. If no egg is released, the woman cannot get pregnant.

> You need to be clear about how the hormones in the menstrual cycle interact with each other. This will help you to answer questions about female fertility, hormonal contraception and assisted reproductive therapy.

Worked example

> To answer this question well, you need to explain where auxin is produced and how it affects cell elongation during plant growth.

The diagram shows an experiment on the effect of one-sided light on plant shoots.

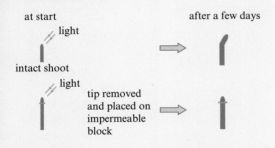

at start   after a few days

light

intact shoot

light

tip removed and placed on impermeable block

Explain the results of the experiment.   **(4 marks)**

The intact shoot grows towards the light. This is because auxin produced in the tip of the shoot moves to the dark side of the shoot, causing more cell elongation there than on the light side.

The shoot on the impermeable block does not grow. This is because auxin produced in the tip of the shoot cannot diffuse to cells below the block and so cannot cause any cell elongation.

Exam practice

1. The table shows the adrenalin concentration in blood samples taken from an athlete just before and at the end of a race.

Time	Just before race	Just after 100 m sprint
adrenalin concentration (mmol/dm³)	0.25	10.2

Explain how the change in adrenalin concentration seen in the table helps the athlete to compete. **(2 marks)**

> **Knowledge check**
>
> Adrenalin is the 'fight or flight' hormone, which has many effects that prepare the body for sudden activity.

2. A germinating seed was planted in the dark so that the young root grew out horizontally. The diagram shows the seedling several days later.

Explain the shape of the root seen in the diagram. **(3 marks)**

> **Knowledge check**
>
> Remember that plant hormones affect growth by changing what happens in cells. Root cells and shoot cells are affected differently by auxin. The change in direction of growth shown in the root is the result of gravitropism.

> ⚠ **Examiner's hint**
>
> You could start this answer by explaining what gravitropism is and how it is caused.

Exam practice

3. Explain why clomifene or similar substances are given to women at the start of IVF treatment. **(4 marks)**

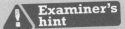

⚠ **Examiner's hint**

A good start to your answer would be to explain what clomifene does.

💡 **Knowledge check**

In IVF (in-vitro fertilisation), eggs are taken out of a woman's ovaries and fertilised with sperm. One or two healthy fertilised eggs are then placed in her uterus to grow.

4. A doctor tests the blood of a patient with a suspected underactive thyroid gland.

Explain why a low concentration of thyroxine and a high concentration of TSH in the blood indicate an underactive thyroid. **(3 marks)**

💡 **Knowledge check**

- A high concentration of thyroxine from the thyroid inhibits the release of TSH from the hypothalamus.

- Reduced release of TSH reduces the amount of TRH released from the pituitary.

- Reduced release of TRH reduces the amount of thyroxine released from the thyroid gland.

85–88

Homeostasis

What's it all about?

Homeostasis is the control of the internal environment of the body, to keep important conditions within safe limits. Examples include thermoregulation, osmoregulation and the control of blood glucose concentration.

Thermoregulation

Thermoregulation is the control of blood temperature to keep key organs (for example, brain and heart) at about 37 °C in humans.

This is important because the optimum temperature for enzymes in these organs is about 37 °C.

Osmoregulation

Osmoregulation controls the water content of the body by adjusting the amount of water excreted in urine. This happens through variation in the secretion of the hormone ADH, which increases the permeability of the collecting duct of the nephron.

Osmoregulation is important because too little water in cells affects their function, and too much water can burst the cell membrane.

Regulation of blood glucose concentration

- Insulin released from the pancreas causes blood glucose concentration to fall.
- Glucagon released from the pancreas causes blood glucose concentration to rise.

Diabetes

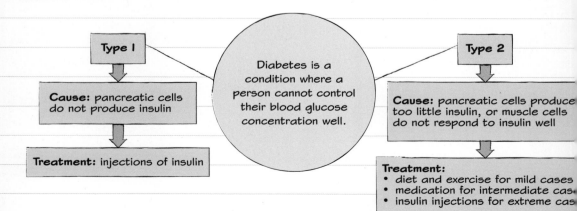

Type 1

Cause: pancreatic cells do not produce insulin

Treatment: injections of insulin

Diabetes is a condition where a person cannot control their blood glucose concentration well.

Type 2

Cause: pancreatic cells produce too little insulin, or muscle cells do not respond to insulin well

Treatment:
- diet and exercise for mild cases
- medication for intermediate cas
- insulin injections for extreme cas

50

Worked example

The graph shows how the relative risk of developing type 2 diabetes varies with BMI for men and women.

Compare and contrast the relationships shown in the graph.   **(2 marks)**

> A good answer to a 'compare and contrast' question will include similarities and differences between the groups mentioned in the question.

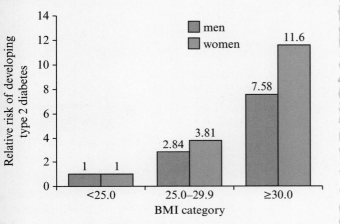

The risk of developing type 2 diabetes increases with increasing BMI in both men and women. The risk for women increases faster with increasing BMI than for men.

Worked example

Explain the role of the hypothalamus in thermoregulation.   **(4 marks)**

The hypothalamus is the part of the brain that monitors temperature. It gets information about internal temperature from receptors that detect temperature changes of the blood. It also receives information about the external temperature from receptors in the skin.

If blood temperature falls too low, the hypothalamus triggers changes in the muscles and skin that help to raise body temperature. If body temperature rises too high, the hypothalamus triggers changes in the skin that help to reduce body temperature.

> This answer focuses on what the hypothalamus does. The answer could describe the changes that happen in the skin and muscles, but this extra information is not asked for in the question.

Exam practice

1. Explain how body temperature is regulated on a hot day.

   (4 marks)

Examiner's hint

Your answer needs to describe two changes in the skin that transfer energy more rapidly from the blood to the environment.

Synoptic link

Remember that capillaries have no muscle cells in their walls, so they cannot change diameter to cause vasodilation or vasoconstriction. This can only happen in arteries.

2. Explain the difference in treatment of type 1 diabetes and type 2 diabetes.

   (4 marks)

Examiner's hint

To answer this well, you will need to link treatment to cause for each type of diabetes

3. Urine tests are often used by doctors to check the function of the kidneys.

   Explain why a doctor would be concerned to find either blood proteins or glucose in a person's urine.   **(4 marks)**

💡 **Knowledge check**

In a healthy person, only small molecules such as water, glucose and ions filter out of blood into the nephron. Glucose is selectively reabsorbed back into the blood from the first convoluted tubule section of the nephron.

4. Explain how concentrated urine is produced by a person on a hot day.   **(4 marks)**

💡 **Knowledge check**

Sweat removes more water from the body on a hot day, so there will be less water in the blood unless more water is drunk.

⚠ **Examiner's hint**

Your answer needs to explain how ADH helps to reduce urine volume and increase its concentration. Remember to include how ADH affects the nephron.

Respiration and circulation

What's it all about?

Blood

Blood consists of:

- liquid plasma (mostly water and dissolved substances)
- red blood cells that carry oxygen
- white blood cells that defend against pathogens
- platelets that help blood to clot.

Blood vessels

The main types of blood vessel are:

- **arteries** – these carry blood away from the heart and have thick muscula walls to prevent bursting
- **capillaries** – these carry blood through tissues and have very thin walls (one cell thick) for rapid exchange of substances between blood and tissues
- **veins** – these carry blood towards th heart and have valves in their walls to prevent backflow.

The heart

Cardiac output is the volume of blood pumped out of the heart in a given time.

$$\text{cardiac output} = \text{stroke volume} \times \text{heart rate}$$

pulmonary artery carries deoxygenated blood to lungs

aorta carries oxygenated blood to body

vena cava brings **deoxygenated blood** from body

pulmonary vein brings oxygenated blood from lungs

right atrium

left atrium

valves prevent blood flowing wrong way through heart **(backflow)**

left ventricle

left ventricle muscle w thicker than right

right ventricle

■ oxygenated blood
■ deoxygenated blood

Respiration

Cellular respiration is an exothermic reaction that transfers energy from the breakdowr of glucose to other metabolic processes. It takes place in mitochondria.

 Aerobic respiration:

- is the complete breakdown of glucose in the presence of oxygen
- produces carbon dioxide and water
- transfers a lot of energy from each molecule of glucose.

 Anaerobic respiration:

- is the incomplete breakdown glucose when oxygen is limite or absent
- transfers less energy from ea glucose molecule
- in muscle cells produces lactic acid – this needs oxygen later convert back to glucose
- in plant and fungal cells produc ethanol and carbon dioxide.

Worked example

The graph shows how body temperature of a mammal and a reptile vary with air temperature.

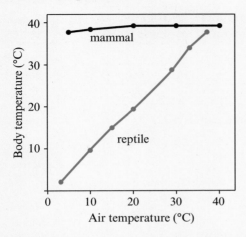

Use information from the graph to explain why most mammalian cells contain many more mitochondria than reptile cells. **(3 marks)**

Mammals keep their body temperature constant at about 37 °C, which means energy is transferred to the environment when the air temperature is lower than this. At lower air temperatures, mammal cells need to release much more energy from the exothermic reaction of respiration than reptile cells. Mitochondria are the sites of respiration in a cell, so more mitochondria allow more respiration.

The graph shows that reptile body temperature is close to air temperature, while mammalian body temperature is maintained above air temperature at about 37 °C. How do mammals do this?

This is a good answer because it describes the relationships shown by the graph between air and body temperature, then gives a reason why the relationship is different for each animal.

Worked example

The adrenalin concentration of an athlete's blood increases just before a race.

Explain the importance of this for the athlete. **(3 marks)**

Adrenalin is the hormone that increases heart rate and breathing rate, and stimulates the liver to release glucose into the blood. These changes increase the rate at which oxygen and glucose are delivered to muscle cells so that they can contract faster when the race begins.

Synoptic link

Adrenalin is the hormone that prepares the body for action, including heart rate and breathing rate.

Exam practice

1. The table shows the effect of a meal on the heart.
   The data are mean values for 25 healthy people.

Time after meal (min)	Cardiac output (cm³/min)	Heart rate (beats/min)	Stroke volume (cm³)
0	4030	62	65
30	5070	65	
120	4092	62	66

Knowledge check

You will need to rearrange the cardiac output equation to calculate stroke volume

(a) Calculate the stroke volume 30 minutes after the meal. **(2 marks)**

Examiner's hint

Remember to show your working in calculation questions.

....

(b) After a meal, blood flow through the capillaries of the stomach and small intestine increases.

Use this information to explain the changes to cardiac output seen in the table. **(3 marks)**

Synoptic link

Your answer should ref to the needs of cells in other parts of the boc to support respiration

2. Towards the end of a marathon race of several hours, athletes often increase their speed and sprint to the end.

Explain how changes in respiration help them to do this. **(2 marks)**

Knowledge check

During most of the race, the athlete will re on aerobic respiration to release the energy needed for muscle contraction. What else can happen in cells to increase the rate of energy release?

xam practice

3. The diagram shows apparatus that can be used to investigate the rate of anaerobic respiration in yeast.

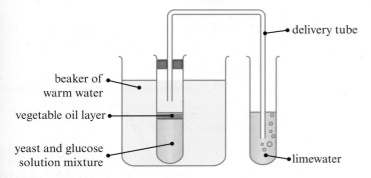

- delivery tube
- beaker of warm water
- vegetable oil layer
- yeast and glucose solution mixture
- limewater

Design an experiment to investigate the rate of anaerobic respiration in yeast, using the apparatus shown in the diagram. **(6 marks)**

💡 **Knowledge check**

Yeast is a fungus.

💡 **Knowledge check**

Limewater goes cloudy as it reacts with carbon dioxide bubbling through it.

Synoptic link

Remember that the reactions of respiration are controlled by enzymes. The rate of enzyme activity is affected by many factors, including temperature, pH and substrate concentration.

If you are asked to design or improve a practical method, you should consider safety, accuracy and repeatability.

💡 **Knowledge check**

A control experiment removes only the intended cause of change, to make sure nothing else is affecting the results.

104–109,
113–115,
117

Organisms and the environment

What's it all about?

Ecosystem terms

- **Trophic level:** feeding level, for example, producer, primary consumer.
- **Interdependence:** how organisms depend on each other for resources such as food and shelter.
- **Biodiversity:** the number of different species of organisms in an area.

Energy transfers

The energy transfers to and from a primary consumer:

energy from respiration transferred to surroundings by heat

energy stored in biomass of food

energy stored in substances in faeces and urine

energy stored as new animal biomass which can be transferred to carnivores in their food

Pyramids of biomass

The food chain for this pyramid is:
lettuce → caterpillar → thrush

thrush | 12 g/m²

caterpillars | 60 g/m²

lettuces | 120 g/m²

1 Pyramids of biomass must start with the producer at the base, with each bar representing the next trophic level in the food chain as you go up the pyramid.

2 Each bar must be drawn to the same scale and shown as a rectangle.

3 Bars must be centred above each other.

Distribution and abundance

Distribution (where organisms live) and **abundance** (how many individuals there are in a population) are affected by:

- **abiotic factors** – non-living factors such as light intensity, temperature, water availability, pollution
- **biotic factors** – factors caused by living organisms such as competition for resources, predator/prey interactions.

Biological cycles

Materials, such as water, carbon and nitrogen, cycle through the abiotic and biotic parts of an ecosystem.

Bacteria play important roles in the nitrogen cycle, including increasing the amount of nitrates available for plant uptake.

Factors may be interrelated. For example, trees reduce the light intensity on the ground below them, and reduce soil moisture and nutrient availability near their roots, but they may also provide shelter for animals.

orked example

Jse the information from the pyramid to explain why here is no predator of thrushes in this food chain.

(3 marks)

The food chain for this pyramid is:
lettuce → caterpillar → thrush

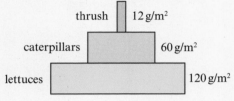

thrush   12 g/m²

caterpillars   60 g/m²

lettuces   120 g/m²

he biomass of 12 g/m² for thrushes means that here is too little energy in that trophic level o support a population of predators that only ats thrushes. This is because the predator ransfers a lot of the energy from its food to he environment by heating or in waste. here will be too little energy left from the food or the predator to store in new biomass.

orked example

tudents planned an investigation to measure how he distribution of snails in an area was related to eight of vegetation.

)escribe a method that could be used for his investigation.

(4 marks)

Quadrats should be placed in areas with lifferent heights of vegetation. For each quadrat, he maximum height of vegetation should be neasured and the number of snails counted.)everal quadrat samples should be taken within ach range of plant height (for example, ranges •f low, medium and tall, as judged from height •f vegetation throughout the area), and a mean hould be calculated for each range to reduce he effect of random variation.

Exam practice

1. (a) A mouse eats a mass of 350 g of wheat grain in
10 days. During that time the mass of the mouse
increases by 6.3 g.

Calculate the energy transfer efficiency between the
grain and the mouse.   **(2 marks)**

Maths
skills

energy transfer efficiency =

$\dfrac{\text{increase in biomass}}{\text{mass of food consumed}} \times 100$

....

(b) The table shows the energy transfer efficiencies
for a fish and a small mammal, which have a
similar biomass and shape.

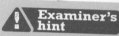

Examiner's
hint

Animal	Main food of animal	Energy transfer efficiency from main food source to animal
freshwater fish (roach)	aquatic plants	7%
small mammal (vole)	land plants	5.2%

Describe a reason for the difference between the
efficiency of energy transfer in the two species.
          (2 marks)

Energy transfer can
affected by:

• how easily the foo
can be digested a
nutrients absorbed

• different ways in
which energy is
transferred from
the animal to the
environment rather
than to biomass.

Surface area to volum
ratio differences can
also affect energy
transfer efficiency, bu
not in this question
because the organism
are of similar shape.

Exam practice

2. A farmer plants three different crops in the same field in three successive years as shown in the table.

Year	Crop
1	wheat
2	beans
3	potatoes

Explain the importance of the bean crop in increasing the yield of potatoes. **(4 marks)**

Knowledge check

Beans, peas and clover are legumes. These plants have roots that develop nodules. Mutualistic, nitrogen-fixing bacteria live inside the nodules.

Mutualistic means that two organisms living in close proximity both benefit from their closeness.

3. Ash trees are the most common trees in many UK woodlands.

Suggest an explanation as to why the communities in those woodlands might change as a result of chalara ash dieback disease. **(4 marks)**

Synoptic link

Ash dieback disease causes leaf loss and can lead to the death of trees.

Examiner's hint

The four marks for this question mean you will need to make four separate points in your answer that describe the impact of interdependence between organisms in a community. Think about which resources will be affected by the loss of trees.

110–112, 116

Human impacts on biodiversity

What's it all about?

Biodiversity

Biodiversity is the variety of species living in an area.

👎 Biodiversity may be reduced by human activities, such as:

- changing land use
- pollution
- introduction of non-indigenous species.

👍 Biodiversity can be maintained through:

- conservation
- reforestation.

Eutrophication

When plant nutrients (for example phosphates and nitrates) are added to water systems (usually by run-off of fertilisers from fields), this can harm biodiversity.

| Eutrophication causes water plants and algae to grow more quickly. | → | Plants and algae cover the water surface and block light to deeper water. | → | Deeper plants cannot get light, so they die. | → | Bacteria decompose dying plants and take oxygen from the water. | → | There is not enough oxygen left in the water for fish, so they die. |

Food security

Food security means providing enough food for everyone to eat. It is challenged by many factors, including an increasing human population, the spread of new pests and pathogens, environmental change such as climate change, and sustainability issues.

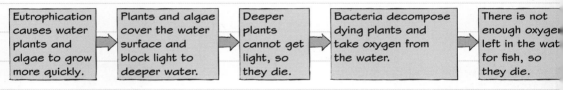

Supplying more food for more people can cause conflict with the needs of other organisms and reduce biodiversi

Pollution indicators

Some organisms are particularly tolerant of, or particularly harmed by, pollution. We can use these organisms as indicators of pollution.

 Air pollution: some lichen species can only grow in clean air, other species can grow in polluted air (for example, by roads); blackspot fungus on roses grows where sulfur pollution is low.

 Water pollution: bloodworms an sludge worms can live in polluted water; freshwater shrimps and stoneflies are only found in clean water.

Worked example

Changes in water quality in a river over time can be studied using
probe that measures oxygen concentration in a sample of water.
They can also be studied by counting the numbers of different
invertebrate species in the water.

Compare and contrast these two methods for assessing
pollution in the river. **(4 marks)**

Oxygen concentration measured by the probe is higher
in unpolluted water and lower in polluted water. This will
show if water is polluted at a particular place and time.
Samples taken at different times will show if pollution is
constant or varies.

The presence or absence of particular invertebrate species
indicates the level of pollution before the sampling. This is
because a change in water quality will affect the survival of
the organisms. This is useful for looking at long-term levels
of pollution in the river.

Worked example

The graph shows the change in sulfur dioxide concentration in
UK air between 1970 and 2016.

Predict, with a reason, the change in occurrence of blackspot
fungus on roses during this period. **(2 marks)**

The fungus is damaged by sulfur dioxide, so the
occurrence of blackspot should have increased a lot as
the amount of sulfur dioxide in the air has fallen.

63

Exam practice

1. The graph shows the changes in mass of fish captured
    globally for human food between 1950 and 2016.

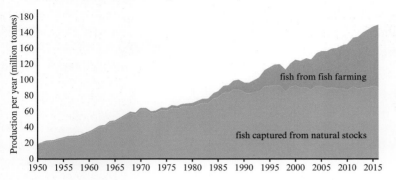

Discuss the importance for biodiversity of the changing
trends in fish production shown in the graph.   **(4 marks)**

2. Maize (sweetcorn) is the main carbohydrate food for
    over 1.2 billion people. Many different varieties used to
    be grown but selective breeding to increase yield means
    that, in the US, only about six closely-related varieties
    are grown.

    Describe the benefits and risks of using selective breeding
    to improve food security.   **(3 marks)**

3. The table shows the mass of nitrogen fertiliser used on crops globally in two different years.

Year	Mass of nitrogen fertiliser (million tonnes)
1961	11.8
2009	102.7

Discuss the benefits and problems of continuing the trend seen in the table.   **(4 marks)**

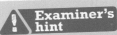

Examiner's hint

Remember to describe the trend as part of the discussion. Your answer needs to consider, in terms of food security, why the trend has happened and why it might need to continue.

Synoptic link

You will need to use your knowledge of the problems caused by fertiliser use to complete your answer.

4. Honey bees are important for the pollination of many crop plants. *Varroa* mites are parasites of honey bees. They suck 'blood' from the bee and can act as a vector for viruses that kill the bees. The mites were originally found only in Asia, but they have been accidentally introduced to many other countries.

Explain the concern for food security as a result of the introduction of *Varroa* to the UK.   **(3 marks)**

Synoptic link

Begin your answer by considering the effect of parasitic mites on bees. Remember that bees and plants share a mutualistic relationship in which both benefit.

Please continue your answer on a separate piece of paper if necessary.

Answers

2–5. Knowledge check

1. B
2. mitochondrion
3. A
4. D
5. C
6. They speed up a reaction.
7. A
8. C
9. energy released from something by burning
10. A
11. A
12. C
13. relay neurone
14. myelin sheath
15. C
16. D
17. C
18. All the genes of an organism.
19. C
20. A version of a gene.
21. red
22. C
23. C
24. D
25. D
26. By (breathing in) bacteria in droplets of mucus coughed out by an infected person.
27. B
28. bacterial infection
29. The risk of developing cardiovascular disease.
30. oxygen
31. C
32. phloem
33. A
34. in blood
35. C
36. A
37. D
38. alveolus / alveoli
39. A
40. B
41. lactic acid
42. B
43. mutualistic / mutualism
44. C
45. B
46. A
47. A

6–9. Cells, division and growth

1. The chloroplasts are in the guard cells surrounding the stomata, but not in the other cells of the leaf surface. **(1)**

   Chloroplasts carry out photosynthesis, so guard cells have lots of sugars for respiration. **(1)**

   Energy from respiration allows the guard cells to change shape, to open and close the stoma. **(1)**

   Stomata are mostly in the lower surface of the leaf, so the other cells have no chloroplasts because most photosynthesis takes place in the upper layers of a leaf. **(1)**

2. total magnification = $10 \times 40 = 400$ **(1)**

   image size = 6.4 cm wide **(1)**

   actual size = $\frac{6.4}{400} = 0.016$ cm **(1)**

   (1 cm = 1000 μm) so answer is 16 μm **(1)**

3. Stem cells are unspecialised cells that can be used to produce all the cells of the immune system. **(1)** Because the stem cells are taken from the patient's body, the new immune system cells they produce will recognise all the other cells of their body **(1)** so they will not attack them. **(1)**

4. In the first 6 months, the boy has a mass that is higher than 50 per cent (half) of all boys of his age. **(1)** In the second 6 months, he has a mass that is higher than 75 per cent of all boys of that age. **(1)** This means his mass has suddenly increased, for example, because he has been eating too much food. **(1)**

–13. Enzymes in action

Any two suitable ways with reasons, for example: use an electronically-controlled water bath **(1)**, because it will keep temperature more constant **(1)**; use a more accurate method to measure the end of the reaction, for example, a colorimeter **(1)**, to give more repeatable results **(1)**; repeat the experiment several times at each pH and find the mean **(1)**, to reduce the effect of random variation and give more repeatable results. **(1)**

Decreasing temperature reduces the rate of enzyme-controlled reactions **(1)**, so processes inside cells – such as respiration to release energy for movement or nerve action – happen more slowly. **(1)**

Juice is released into the small intestine. **(1)** Proteases break down proteins in food to amino acids for absorption. **(1)** Amylase breaks down starch to glucose for absorption. **(1)** Substances with a high pH neutralise acid from the stomach to provide the optimum pH for enzyme action. **(1)** rate of digestion $= \frac{1.0}{340} = 0.0029$ **(1)** $=$ 2.9×10^{-3} g/s **(1)**

(max. 1 mark if answer isn't in standard form; both marks for correct standard form answer without working)

–17. Getting into and out of cells

$\frac{11.71 - 14.26}{14.26} \times 100$ **(1)**

$= -17.88\%$ **(1)**

1 mark only if answer not given to 2 d.p

To gain full marks, your answer must be clearly written in a logical structure. It must also show understanding of the scientific ideas involved, including some of the points shown below. Your answer must describe and explain the roles of breathing **and** of blood flow in gas exchange. **(6)**

Breathing
- draws air into the lungs from the outside
- providing a higher concentration of oxygen in the alveoli than in the blood
- so oxygen diffuses into the blood from air in the alveoli
- expels air from the lungs to the outside
- providing a lower concentration of carbon dioxide in the alveoli than in the blood
- so carbon dioxide diffuses out of the blood into the alveoli

Blood flow
- alveoli have closely associated capillaries

- blood flow brings blood with a higher concentration of carbon dioxide and lower oxygen concentration to the alveoli
- maintains a steep concentration gradient for carbon dioxide and oxygen
- a steep concentration gradient maximises the rate of diffusion of gases between blood and air

3. (a)
$$\frac{SA}{V} = \frac{(2 \times 5 \times 1) + (2 \times 5 \times 0.4) + (2 \times 1 \times 0.4)}{5 \times 1 \times 0.4}$$

$$= \frac{14.8}{2.0} \text{ (1)}$$

$= 7.4\,\text{mm}^3$ **(1)** *(both marks for the correct final answer without working)*

(b) The flatworm has a large SA : V ratio because it is very thin/flat. **(1)** This means there is only a short distance for substances to diffuse between the environment and the tissues in the flatworm's body. **(1)** The rate of diffusion across this short distance is fast enough to support all processes needed for life. **(1)**

4. During the day, plants need to absorb carbon dioxide from the air to make sugars through photosynthesis. **(1)** The carbon dioxide diffuses into the leaves through the open stomata. **(1)** At night, there is no photosynthesis so no need for carbon dioxide, so the stomata close **(1)** to prevent unnecessary diffusion of water molecules out of the leaves. **(1)**

18–21. The nervous system

1. The reflex response is rapid because it only involves three neurones: a sensory neurone, a relay neurone in the spinal cord and a motor neurone. **(1)** It involves no conscious thought from the brain because the response is triggered directly by the stimulus. **(1)** This rapid unconscious response helps to protect the light-receiving cells in the eye from damage that might be caused by bright light. **(1)**

2. A synapse is where neurones meet, and where a neurotransmitter carries the nerve impulse across the gap between the neurones by diffusion. **(1)** A chemical neurotransmitter is only released from the neurone before the synapse, so the nerve impulse can only travel in one direction through the nervous system. **(1)** Many neurones may meet at a synapse, so the impulse from one neurone can be spread rapidly to many other neurones. **(1)**

3. A patient is injected with the radioactive substance which attaches to any amyloid in their brain. **(1)** A PET scan is used to identify where the radioactive substance has attached

to amyloid. **(1)** The amount of amyloid in the brain may indicate whether or not the person is developing Alzheimer's disease. **(1)**

4. Long-sightedness is caused by the image/light rays being focused behind the retina. **(1)** A converging lens will bend the light rays before they enter the eye so that they focus on the retina. **(1)**

22–25. DNA and protein synthesis

1. C **(1)**

2. HIV viruses replicate by making the human cell produce new viral proteins. **(1)**

   The HIV viruses do this by inserting their DNA into human DNA and causing transcription to form mRNA and translation to form the viral proteins. **(1)**

   As the drug prevents viral DNA inserting into human DNA, no viral proteins will be produced. **(1)**

3. Each protein has a particular sequence of amino acids. **(1)**

   The sequence of amino acids in a protein is produced from a particular sequence of bases on an mRNA strand during translation. **(1)**

   The base sequence of the mRNA strand is produced by complementary pairing with bases on a DNA strand. **(1)**

   This allows that particular base sequence to be identified in the genome. **(1)**

4. A mutation in the gene could change the amino acid sequence that is produced after transcription and translation. **(1)**

   The changed amino acid sequence will fold up in a different shape. **(1)**

   This could change the shape of the active site of the enzyme so that phenylalanine no longer fits into it. **(1)**

26–29. Genetics and variation

1. The alleles used in the answer should be defined, for example, I^A = A allele, I^B = B allele and I^o = O allele.

		Father's alleles	
		I^A	I^o
Mother's alleles	I^B	$I^A I^B$	$I^B I^o$
	I^o	$I^A I^o$	$I^o I^o$

(1 mark for correct parent alleles, 1 mark for correct offspring genotypes)

The genotype $I^A I^B$ produces the phenotype blood group AB because the alleles are codominant. **(1)**

The probability of a child with the $I^A I^B$ genotype is 1 in 4 / 25% / ratio 1 : 3 **(1)**

2. Normal colour vision male. **(1)** Person A has a daughter with normal vision who is not a carrier so A's X chromosome must not have the colour-blindness allele. **(1)**

3. Mendel's results showed that the phenotypes of the first generation were always either yellow seeds or green seeds: there was no mixing of the two. **(1)**

   The results also show an approximate 3 : 1 ratio offspring phenotypes in the second generation.

   This can only be explained by the parents having two identical copies of the particle (gene) for the phenotype **(1)**; all offspring in the first generation having one yellow seed particle (gene) and one green seed particle (gene); and the 2nd generation offspring having a ratio of 1 with two yellow seed particles (genes) : 2 with one yellow seed and one green seed particle (gene) : 1 with two green seed particles (genes). **(1)**

4. (Using Y for the yellow allele and y for the white allele), if the plant is homozygous:

		Yellow flowers	
		Y	Y
White flowers	y	Yy	Yy
	y	Yy	Yy

All/100 per cent of the plants produced from the cross will have yellow flowers. **(1)**

If the plant is heterozygous:

		Yellow flowers	
		Y	y
White flowers	y	Yy	yy
	y	Yy	yy

Half/50 per cent of the plants produced from the cross will have white flowers. **(1)**

30–33. Evolution and classification

1. Penicillin kills most staph bacteria. **(1)**

   Variation between staph bacteria means some bacteria are resistant to the effects of penicillin, and so survive. **(1)**

   The resistant bacteria then divide to produce colonies of penicillin-resistant staph bacteria, resulting in evolution of the staph bacteria. **(1)**

2. Both moles live in the same kind of environment. **(1)**

Adaptations to that environment (for example, body shape and size) cause their skeletons to look similar. **(1)**

DNA analysis is better at showing evolutionary relationships because similarities in DNA have come through inheritance. **(1)**

Both theories show the effect of the environment on the evolution of species **(1)** and of competition between individuals of the same species for limited resources. **(1)**

Lamarck's theory says that characteristics which change (are acquired) in an individual's life can be passed on to their offspring. **(1)** Darwin's theory says that genes/alleles which produce characteristics that increase the chance of survival are passed on to offspring. **(1)**

Any two suitable reasons **(2)**, such as:

- there is no DNA evidence from bones to show how closely related the two species are genetically
- there may be another species we have not found yet that is the direct ancestor
- there was a long time between Lucy (3.2 million years) and *Homo habilis* (1.6 million years) so there may be other species between them.

–37. Genetic engineering and ⌐lective breeding

Grain yield using GM maize increases by about 10 per cent while crop damage decreases by about ⌐65 per cent and pest population size decreases by about 85 per cent. **(1)**

Crop damage decreases because there are fewer ⌐rootworms causing the damage. **(1)**

Yield increases because less damage means the ⌐plants grow better / produce more food. **(1)**

Many plants can be produced **(1)** and the process ⌐is quicker than breeding. **(1)** The plants will be ⌐genetically identical owing to mitosis, so they will ⌐all produce the artemisinin. **(1)**

To gain full marks, your answer must be clearly ⌐written in a logical structure. It must also show ⌐understanding of the scientific ideas involved, ⌐including some of the points shown below. Your answer must include at least two benefits ⌐and one risk, giving reasons why they are helpful ⌐or problematic. **(6)**

Benefits

- Increase in body weight gain from 22 g to 50 g per animal per year.
- More chicken meat can be produced from fewer chickens.
- Growers have more meat to sell.

- There is more chicken meat available for sale in the same time period.
- Decrease in mass of feed from 4.1 kg to 1.7 kg per kg increase in body mass.
- Grower gets more meat for less feed which could make it cheaper to grow chicken.

Risks

- Animals that grow so quickly could have physical problems, such as not being able to move about easily, or heart problems due to moving a much larger body mass.
- Animals producing much more meat for less food may not get enough food to support other tissues well, such as strong bones.

4. Time taken to affect pests and so reduce damage: Chemicals/insecticides are likely to have an immediate effect but parasites will take time to kill pests. **(1)**

   Number of applications needed to control pests: Chemicals may need to be applied several times because they may break down in the environment, while parasites may only need to be applied once. **(1)**

   Impact on the environment: Chemicals may poison many insect species and so affect the biodiversity of their predators, but parasites target only caterpillars so they have less impact on other insects. **(1)**

   Cost of control and application: Different methods of control need different methods and timing of applications, which will affect cost. **(1)**

38–41. Health, disease and medicine

1. Antigens from the cancer cells are injected into a mouse **(1)** so the mouse makes lymphocytes that produce antibodies to the antigens. **(1)** Lymphocytes from the mouse are fused with cancer cells to form hybridoma cells that continue to grow and divide. **(1)** Antibodies made by the hybridoma cells are attached to a cancer-killing drug. **(1)**

2. Having the same BMI suggests a similar risk of dying from cardiovascular disease. **(1)** However, man A has a waist:hip ratio above 1.0, while man B has a waist:hip ratio that is below 1.0. **(1)** So, man A has more fat around his waist than man B and therefore has a higher risk of dying from cardiovascular disease. **(1)**

3. The equipment and agar should be prepared in an autoclave where the high temperature will kill any microorganisms. **(1)** The culture bottle and inoculating loop should be passed through a Bunsen flame before inoculating the plate to kill

microorganisms in the air and on the loop. **(1)** The lid of the Petri dish should be held above the plate during inoculation to stop microorganisms falling onto the agar. **(1)**

4. If most people are immunised, then the chance of anyone in the population having measles is very low. **(1)** This means there is a very low chance of a non-immunised child coming into contact with an infected person. **(1)**

5. You would look at the clear zone around each disc. The one with the wider clear zone is better at killing the bacteria. **(1)**

42–45. Photosynthesis and transport

1. To gain full marks, your answer must be clearly written in a logical structure. It must also show understanding of the scientific ideas involved, including some of the points shown below. Your answer must give a reason for each improvement you describe, and should include at least three improvements. **(6)**

   Improvements
   - Use the same volume of indicator solution in each bottle / use the same size (or mass) of algal ball in each bottle.
   - Screw the tops back on bottles as soon as the balls have been added.
   - Measure distances with a ruler / with the bottles placed in the same way (for example, front edge of bottle aligned with distance mark).
   - Repeat the experiment several times and calculate a mean for each distance.

   Reasons
   - Same volume or mass ensures that the dilution of gas released from the balls is the same.
   - Screwing the tops back on prevents carbon dioxide in the air affecting the indicator solution.
   - Measuring in this way makes the distances as accurate as possible.
   - Repeating and taking the mean reduces the effect of random variation in the results.

2. The distance has doubled, so the number of bubbles will be reduced in proportion to $\frac{1}{2^2} = \frac{1}{4}$ **(1)**
   $60 \times \frac{1}{4} = 15$ bubbles per minute **(1)**

3. Any suitable set-up that reduces wind movement to zero with the least possible impact on other factors, such as:
   - place an identical potted plant in a transparent plastic bag and seal it **(1)** (so it is not affected by the fan)

- place the bagged plant next to the experiment plant for the 24 hours **(1)** (so that light and temperature for both plants are the same).

4. Increasing temperature from 20 °C to 30 °C increases the rate of growth **(1)** because reaction that build new cells can happen faster when molecules have more energy. **(1)** Increasing the carbon dioxide concentration from 0.04% to 0.14% increases the rate of growth **(1)** because carbon dioxide is a reactant/substrate for photosynthesis and more reactant/substrate means more photosynthesis reactions can happen at the same time. **(1)**

46–49. Hormones in animals and plants

1. Adrenalin stimulates an increase in heart rate, breathing rate and blood glucose concentration. These changes deliver oxygen and glucose to muscles more quickly so that they can work harder or faster in the race. **(1)**

2. Auxin collected in the lower side of the root as grew out from the seed. **(1)** Higher concentratio of auxin inhibit cell elongation in roots. **(1)** So the cells on the upper side of the root grew long than those on the lower side, causing the root ti to bend downwards. **(1)**

3. Clomifene is given to women to stimulate their pituitary gland to release more FSH and LH. **(** FSH stimulates eggs to mature in the ovaries **(1** and LH stimulates ovulation. **(1)** This means there should be several mature eggs to collect from the ovaries for fertilisation outside the woman's body in IVF. **(1)**

4. An underactive thyroid gland will release less thyroxine than normal into the blood, causing the low concentration. **(1)** A low concentration of thyroxine in the blood will stimulate the hypothalamus to release more TRH. **(1)** More TRH will stimulate the pituitary to relea more TSH into the blood, causing the high concentration. **(1)**

50–53. Homeostasis

1. If body temperature rises, the hypothalamus triggers the release of sweat from sweat glands onto the surface of the skin. **(1)** Energy transfer from the body to the water in sweat helps to coo the skin surface when it evaporates. **(1)**

   The hypothalamus also instructs the muscle in artery walls in the dermis / the shunt vessel to constrict, increasing blood flow through capillaries near the skin surface. **(1)** This allow energy from the blood to be transferred more quickly to the air. **(1)**

Type 1 diabetes can only be treated with injections of insulin (1) because the pancreas no longer produces insulin in response to high blood glucose concentration. (1) Type 2 diabetes can often be treated by a low-carbohydrate diet and exercise to help keep blood glucose concentration low (1) because the pancreas does not produce enough insulin to cope with a rapid rise in blood glucose concentration. (1)

The presence of blood proteins in urine indicates that something has gone wrong with the filtering of blood as it passes through the glomerulus (1) because blood proteins are too large to pass through the filter. (1)

The presence of glucose in urine suggests there is too much glucose in the blood / something wrong with the reabsorption of glucose in the first convoluted tubule (1) because normally all glucose that filters into the nephron is selectively reabsorbed back into the blood. (1)

A hot day leads to sweating and loss of water. (1) Reduced water content of the blood triggers the pituitary gland to release ADH into the blood. (1) ADH increases the permeability of the collecting duct of the nephrons in the kidneys. (1) This makes it easier for water to move out of the filtrate in the nephron into the kidney tissue and blood by osmosis. (1)

4–57. Respiration and circulation

(a) stroke volume = $\dfrac{\text{cardiac output}}{\text{heart rate}} = \dfrac{5070}{65}$ (1) = 78 cm^3 (1)

(b) Cardiac output increases after a meal so more blood flows around the body in a given time. (1) This helps make sure that other parts of the body get sufficient blood while there is increased flow in the stomach and intestine. (1) Sufficient blood is needed to deliver the oxygen and glucose that all cells need for respiration and to remove waste carbon dioxide produced during respiration. (1)

Anaerobic respiration in cells releases additional energy for the sprint without the need for extra oxygen. (1) This happens in addition to the aerobic respiration that has been happening in muscle cells since the race began. (1)

To gain full marks, your answer must be clearly written in a logical structure. It must also show understanding of the scientific ideas involved, including some of the points shown below.
Your answer must clearly describe the stages of the experiment and show how the way each stage is carried out helps to produce useful results (To a maximum of 6 marks):

- Set up a control experiment – the same but without any yeast – to show that bubbles produced are caused by yeast and not by another part of the apparatus.
- Set up the experiment, changing one variable – for example, using different concentrations of sugar solution, or changing the temperature of the water bath so that any change can be clearly attributed to the changed variable.
- Keep all other variables the same (for example, volume of sugar solution, amount of yeast, room temperature) so that any change in results is clearly attributable to changes in the independent variable.
- Use a colorimeter (or other more accurate measure of turbidity than by eye) to judge the end point in each test more consistently.
- Repeat the experiments and calculate a mean for each result to improve accuracy and reduce the effects of random variation.
- Wear eye protection to protect eyes when working with liquids.
- Wash hands thoroughly after handling microorganisms.

58–61. Organisms and the environment

1. (a) $\dfrac{6.3}{350} \times 100$ (1) = 1.8% (1)

   (b) Any suitable answer that provides a valid reason for the difference, such as:
   - the land plants that the vole eats may be more difficult to digest than the aquatic plants that the fish eats (1) so a smaller proportion of the nutrients in the food will be absorbed into the vole's body than into the fish's body (1)
   - voles are warm-blooded but fish are not (1) so the vole will transfer more of the energy from its food to the environment by heating and there will be less energy for making more vole biomass. (1)

2. Beans have root nodules containing nitrogen-fixing bacteria. (1) The bacteria convert nitrogen in the air into nitrogen compounds in the bean roots. (1) Some of these nitrogen compounds will become available to the potato plants in the next year, when the bean roots naturally decompose (beans are annual plants). (1) Plants need nitrogen compounds to make proteins for healthy growth. (1)

3. Any suitable answer that provides reasons for suggested changes, such as:
   - ash dieback disease will cause loss of leaves on the ash trees and may kill the trees (1)

- loss of leaves will increase the amount of light getting to plants growing below the trees **(1)**, which may increase their rate of growth as they will photosynthesise more **(1)**
- death of trees may reduce food availability and shelter for animals (for example, birds) so their abundance will decrease **OR** death of trees will provide more food for decomposers and the animals that eat them, so their abundance will increase. **(1)**

62–65. Human impacts on biodiversity

1. The answer should clearly link changing fish capture trends to impact on biodiversity. This can be done in several ways:

   The total mass of fish captured is increasing to help feed an increasing human population. **(1)** However, the mass of fish captured from wild stocks has remained fairly constant since about 1988 **(1)**, so the increase in supply of fish from fish farming means that natural fish stocks are not being reduced further to supply human food. **(1)** This helps to protect biodiversity in communities that include the wild fish because they are not being removed from the food web. **(1)**

   OR The total mass of fish captured is increasing to help feed an increasing human population. **(1)** However, the mass of fish captured from wild stocks has remained fairly constant since about 1988, which may be because many wild stocks have been overfished. **(1)** Not increasing

wild stock fishing will help to maintain the biodiversity that is left **(1)**, though providing foo for farmed fish from wild fish stocks could still harm biodiversity in the wild. **(1)**

2. Selective breeding can improve the characteristics of a crop species so that it produces more food to support a growing human population. **(1)** Selective breeding also reduces genetic variation within a crop variety and between varieties that are developed from one another. **(1)** If only those varieties are grown, limited genetic variation will make the all susceptible to the same pests or pathogens, which means large amounts of crop could be destroyed at the same time. **(1)**

3. The mass of nitrogen fertiliser used was nearly 10 times greater in 2009 than in 1961. **(1)** This increase has made it possible to increase the yie of crops to provide more food for a growing human population. **(1)** Increased use of fertilise also increases the risk of eutrophication of rive and lakes **(1)**, which increases the risk of harm the organisms living in those lakes and rivers, a so may reduce biodiversity. **(1)**

4. The parasitic mites harm and may kill honey bees. **(1)** Many crop plants depend on pollinatio to reproduce, forming new plants and the parts that provide us with food (such as fruit and vegetables). **(1)** If the number of honey bees decreases, then less food will be produced, whic risks food security. **(1)**

Match to the Revise Pearson Edexcel GCSE (9–1) Combined Science Higher Revision Guide

you are taking the Pearson Edexcel GCSE (9–1) Combined Science Higher exam
e the table below to match the pages and knowledge check questions to the
evise Pearson Edexcel GCSE (9–1) Combined Science Higher Revision Guide.
ne circled knowledge check questions are Pearson Edexcel GCSE (9–1) Biology
gher only questions.

ail it! Biology pages	Knowledge check question	Combined Science RG pages
–9	1, 2, 3, 4, 5, 16	1–6, 13–16, 20
0–13	6, 7	7–9, 63
4–17	10, 11	10–11, 56, 66–67
8–21	⑫, 13, 14, ⑮	17–18
2–25	17, 18, ⑲	21
6–29	20, 21, 22	22–27
0–33	23	29–31
4–37	24	32–34
8–41	25, 26, 27, 28, 29	36–48
2–45	30, 31, 32	50–56
6–49	33, 34, 35	58–62
0–53	36	63–64
4–57	㉟, 39, 40, 41	67–74
8–61	42, 43, ㊹, 45, 46	76–80, 83–85
2–65	47	81–82

Notes

Notes

Notes

Notes

Published by Pearson Education Limited, 80 Strand, London, WC2R 0RL.

www.pearsonschoolsandfecolleges.co.uk

Copies of official specifications for all Pearson qualifications may be found on the website:
qualifications.pearson.com

Text and illustrations © Pearson Education Limited 2019
Typeset by Newgen KnowledgeWorks Pvt. Ltd., Chennai, India
Produced and illustrated by Newgen Publishing UK
Cover illustration © Miriam Sturdee

The right of Sue Kearsey to be identified as author of this work has been asserted by her in accordance with the
Copyright, Designs and Patents Act 1988.

First published 2019

22 21 20 19
10 9 8 7 6 5 4 3 2 1

British Library Cataloguing in Publication Data
A catalogue record for this book is available from the British Library

ISBN 978 1 292 29426 1

Printed in Slovakia by Neografia.

Acknowledgements
Content written by Pauline Lowrie is included.

Text Credits

Pg 36: Ellegrino, Elisa; Bedini, Stefano; Nuti, Marco and Ercoli, Laura. Impact of genetically engineered maize
on agronomic, environmental and toxicological traits: a meta-analysis of 21 years of field data, *Scientific Reports*
8:3113, DOI:10.1038/s41598-018-21284. Material is licensed under a Creative Commons CC-BY Attribution 4.0
International Licence; **Pg 37:** Arthur, James and Albers, Gerard AA. Detail taken from Figure 1: Increase of
efficiency of meat production in pigs and poultry over four decades calculated for the entire life of the animal from
birth to slaughter in 'Industrial Perspective on Problems and Issues Associated with Poultry Breeding'.
Poultry Genetics, Breeding and Biotechnology (eds W.M. Muir and S.E. Aggrey) © CAB International 2003.
Reproduced with permission of the Licensor through PLSclear; **Pg 51:** Langenberg et al. Data from 'Long-Term
Risk of Incident Type 2 Diabetes and Measures of Overall and Regional Obesity: The EPIC-InterAct
Case-Cohort Study. The InterAct Consortium'. *PLoS Medicine*, 5 June 2012, Volume 9, Issue 6, e1001230.
The InterAct Consortium (2012). Material is licensed under a Creative Commons CC-BY Attribution 4.0
International Licence; **Pg 63:** Department For Environment, Food And Rural Affairs. Emissions of air pollutants in
the UK, 1970 to 2017. https://assets.publishing.service.gov.uk/government/uploads/system/uploads/attachment_data/
file/778483/Emissions_of_air_pollutants_1990_2017.pdf, © DEFRA/Crown Copyright, 2018. Contains public sector
information licensed under the Open Government Licence v3.0; **Pg 64:** Food and Agriculture Organisation of the
United Nations. Fig 1, p3 WORLD CAPTURE FISHERIES AND AQUACULTURE PRODUCTION. The State
of world fisheries and aquaculture 2018 – Meeting the sustainable development goals (Rome).
http://www.fao.org/3/i9540en/i9540en.pdf, © FAO, 2018. Reproduced with permission.

Notes from the publisher

1. While the publishers have made every attempt to ensure that advice on the qualification and its assessment is
accurate, the official specification and associated assessment guidance materials are the only authoritative source of
information and should always be referred to for definitive guidance.

Pearson examiners have not contributed to any sections in this resource relevant to examination papers for which
they have responsibility.

2. Pearson has robust editorial processes, including answer and fact checks, to ensure the accuracy of the content in
this publication, and every effort is made to ensure this publication is free of errors. We are, however, only human,
and occasionally errors do occur. Pearson is not liable for any misunderstandings that arise as a result of errors in
this publication, but it is our priority to ensure that the content is accurate. If you spot an error, please do contact us
at resourcescorrections@pearson.com so we can make sure it is corrected.